GLIMMERINGS AND CONSTELLATIONS

Critical and Creative Responses

Selected Plays of Jay Wright, Volume 3

Edited by Will Daddario

Kenning Editions / *Every house has a door* 2024

Glimmerings and Constellations: Creative and Critical Responses
Selected Plays of Jay Wright, Volume 3

ISBN: 979-8-9856628-4-9
LCCN: 2023937873

Will Daddario, project editor

Cover design: Crisis
Interior design: Cory Rockliff

Published in Chicago by
Kenning Editions and *Every house has a door*

Distributed by
Small Press Distribution, Berkeley, CA: Spdbooks.org

This book was made possible in part by
the subscribers and supporters of Kenning Editions.

Every house has a door gratefully acknowledges support for this
publication by The MacArthur Funds for Art and Culture at
the Richard H. Driehaus Foundation, and the generosity of
individual donors.

Kenningeditions.com
Everyhousehasadoor.org

0 Jay Wright's Theater: Some Sounds from These Sights 5
Will Daddario

1 Seven Dramaturgical Notes on *Passage* 45
Matthew Goulish

2 What I See in *Homage to Anthony Braxton* 59
Devin King

3 Blues Restructuralism: Jay Wright's
Homage to Anthony Braxton 75
David Grubbs

4 Collective Silence in *The Delights of Memory* 89
Michael Paul Berlin

5 No Redemption: Fate and Limbo in
The Delights of Memory 95
Esteban Rodríguez

6 Disappearance, Disappearing, Disappeared 105
Sebastián Calderón Bentin

7 The Radical Performance of Getting Lost: Multiplicity
in *The Possible Impossibility of Leaving Home* 113
Daniel Woody

8 *Lemma*: Jay Wright's Idiorrhythmic American Theater 133
Will Daddario

9 Code: A Sport (Approaching Jay Wright)
A Drama 159
Duriel E. Harris

JAY WRIGHT'S THEATER

Some Sounds from These Sights

Will Daddario

CONSTELLATIONS AND GLIMMERINGS

HISTORIANS SING of the impossible Dogon knowledge of the star known as Sirius B. The binary partner of Sirius (Σείριος, "scorching"), named as such by the Ancient Greeks who noted the heliacal rise of the star at the beginning of the season of the greatest heat, played a centrally important role in the cosmology of the Ancient Dogon people, a fact which seems unremarkable given the importance of stars to so many civilizations, until, that is, we grapple with the fact that Western astronomers knew nothing of Sirius B until 1844. In that year, Friedrich Wilhelm Bessel surmised the existence of Sirius B by deducing that another star must be exerting sufficient gravitational force upon Sirius—the Dog Star of the Canis Major constellation—to induce its unusual, wobbly movement. The American Alvan Clark confirmed Bessel's hunch in 1862 when his new telescope was able to lay eyes on Sirius B. Western astronomers thus came to confirm the existence of the star, calculate its immense mass (i.e., roughly the same mass of our Sun packed into a body roughly the volume of our Earth), and chart its mutual orbit with Sirius, an orbit that takes 50 Earth years to complete. How, then, without any telescopic visual confirmation or indeed any trace of the star in the sky, did the Dogon know of Sirius B, seemingly millennia before Bessel? How did they know of its 50-year orbital dance with its twin and its immense mass? This is why historians sing of the Dogon knowledge of Sirius B. It seems, to put it mildly, impossible.

It's not impossible. The question, rather, is one of knowledge. What constitutes "knowing"? How does one come to know? For the Ancient Dogon, according to the studies compiled by French anthropologists Marcel Griaule and Germaine Dieterlen, knowledge is an assemblage of material forces. Water, word, threads, and woven fabric, for example, make knowledge possible within the Dogon mytho-history; indeed, those elements are coextensive with knowledge itself. These elements were carried to the Dogon people by a race of beings called the Nommo, themselves fabricated by Amma, the creator, and the stories of creation were inscribed in the stars.

To know, then, is to read the stitchwork that unites the seemingly disparate materials and energies of the terrestrial and extraterrestrial worlds. Rhythm is the translation of celestial fire pounded out by the blacksmith's art. How does one know rhythm? By allowing one's body to speak that translation. The four cardinal directions evolved from the dismembered bodies of the Nommo. How does one come to know these directions and the sacrifice of the Nommo? Through rituals formed around ancestor veneration and absorption in the radiance of the number four. At no point does possibility or impossibility enter the picture. The picture, instead, begins to form through a performance of rhythm and number, two concepts (percepts? affects?) that draw their energy from the stars.

Readers familiar with the poetry of Jay Wright will understand why I have started here. The Dogon, as well as the neighboring Bamana, loom large in his oeuvre. Ogotemmêli, the Dogon elder who imparted his people's knowledge to Griaule, for example, appears as the focal point of Part IV in Wright's 1976 volume *Soothsayers and Omens*:

> But your voice comes clearly
> only where I found you,
> and so I come again
> into these mountains,
> and scrape the narrow streets and pyramids,
> to find you, robed in brown,

> perched on a stone,
> pinching your leather snuffbox. [...]¹

And again, like a neutrino in the Wright multiverse, he pops onto a page of *The Prime Anniversary* (2019):

> Ogotemmêli stands on his own green terrace.
> The lines and planes of that garden should remind him
> of imaginary things, no finite and slim
> number of his body's diagram, or slow pace
> of a logical relation tuned in Athens.²

Wright also summons Dogon cosmology directly in the title and structure of his works. The eight books of poetry collected in the volume *Transfigurations* (2000) represent the eight Dogon master signs, specific symbols that orient one within the Dogon universe. *The Guide Signs, Book One and Book Two* (2007) name additional symbols in that same lexicon/symbology and represent the primordial Nommo twins, such that, collectively, these ten books of Wright's poetry "provide the base for the soul and life force given to everything," just like the collected 266 signs within the Dogon symbolic system.³

As for the Bamana, also known as the Bambara, we feel their presence in, to name only a couple instances, the title of Wright's 1980 *The Double Invention of Komo* and, closer to the present moment, the cover images on this volume and the two volumes of selected plays titled *The Dramatic Radiance of Number* and *Figurations and Dedications* (2022). The Antelope headdresses on the covers of these three books are masks featured in the Bamana's Chi (or Ci) Wara performances, which "encourage Bamana farmers as they work in the fields and praise

---

1 Wright, *Transfigurations: Collected Poems* (Baton Rouge, LA: Louisiana State University Press, 2000), 137.

2 Wright, *The Prime Anniversary* (Chicago: Flood Editions, 2019), 14.

3 This comes from the back jacket of Wright, *The Guide Signs: Book One and Book Two* (Baton Rouge, LA: Louisiana State University Press, 2007).

their efforts after they have returned to the village when the work is complete."[4] Wright's plays—and also his poetry—call to mind precisely this kind of commemoration: song and dance delivered on the occasion of work completed in the fields, where "the fields" refer to the itineraries of the everyday and "work" refers to the task of living. It is worth noting that Jay and Lois Wright, together, selected the images for these covers. The cover of vol. 1, accordingly, showcases the male antelope mask and invites readers into plays selected by Jay. The cover on vol. 2 showcases the female antelope (carrying a fawn) and invites readers into plays selected by Lois. The cover of this book, vol. 3, offers an antelope mask from the Marka people of northwest Mali, chosen by Wright for the way it conveys both masculine and feminine properties.

The title of this volume, *Glimmerings and Constellations*, intends to recognize Wright's affinity for the Dogon, Bamana, and other African peoples, generally, as well as, more specifically, his ability to read the stars and report on his findings:

> In a morning coat,
> hands locked behind your back,
> you walk gravely along the lines in your head.
> These others stands with you,
> squinting the city into place,
> yet cannot see what you see,
> what you would see
> —a vision of these paths,
> laid out like a star,
> or like a body,
> the seed vibrating within itself,
> breaking into the open,
> dancing up to stop at the end of the universe.[5]

4 *Headdress: Male Antelope* (*Ci Wara*), 19th–early 20th c., Metropolitan Museum of Art, New York, https://www.metmuseum.org/art/collection/search/310864.

5 Wright, "Benjamin Banneker Helps to Build a City," *Transfigurations*, 103.

These lines from "Benjamin Banneker Helps to Build a City" (1976) paint a picture of the free Black man who helped to design the plan for Washington, DC, but whose presence is typically omitted from the telling of the capital city's birth. I also think of Wright when I read these lines. Both Banneker and he survey a great expanse and materialize a grand design that roots itself in the Earth but takes its rhythmic pulsation from the quintessence of star power. Both Banneker and he are great architects of this country's soul and imagination. Both Banneker and he are too frequently left off the list of those whose imagination protects our collective light from dimming.

Starlight guides the title of this volume because it appears throughout Wright's oeuvre. Here are a few examples:

> A clock makes itself
> of precious metals and glass
> and a damaged star.[6]

> All summer connotations fill this light
> a symmetry of different scales—the site
> of fibrous silence, the velvet lace
> of iris, alders the moon can ignite.
> One feels the amplitude of grief, the pace
> of oscillating stars, power in place
> where time has crossed and left a breathy stain. [...][7]

> The altar dances upon its star,
>   secure in its orbit.
> Say that the dervish Dog Star dances
> upon its altar.
> You cannot sing that song, or thread
> a corollary music
> through impeccable orbits. [...][8]

6 *Prime Anniversary*, 26.
7 Wright, "Light's Interrupted Amplitude," in *Guide Signs*, 64.
8 *Guide Signs*, 110.

This flower must have known
the salt glint of sand,
the bedouin billow of wind,
the lapis lazuli stars that rise

when the desert's sea voice stops.
Now it sits, singularly crimson,
near the toucan and anaconda.[9]

Day by day,
from west to east,
the earth rotates on its axis
and the stars,
going against the grain,
shimmy around the one point
    that seems fixed.
So I know a star stand
when I know where I stand,
linked by that sphere to my own earth.

[...]

There is trouble here with the eye,
or the body adapting to a different
    Latitude,
that moment when we know
a star forever invisible,
the body closed upon its own desire.[10]

The phrase "glimmerings and constellations" speaks, then, to the role the stars play in Wright's thought, but also to the fringes of knowledge, the corners only sometimes lit, the line of sight enabled, at night, by stars both visible and as yet unseen. Some of the blinking objects in

9 Wright, "Passionflower," from *Elaine's Book*, in *Transfigurations*, 472.
10 Wright, "10," from *Boleros*, in *Transfigurations*, 506.

the constellations may be stars, others may be planets, and others
as-yet-unfathomable celestial bodies whose light speaks in languages
we do not yet understand. The essays and creative responses collected
in this volume will hopefully provide some insight into the workings
of Wright's theatrical offerings. They do not completely decode the
symbology of Wright's dramatic work—of course, how could they?
Nevertheless, they are here to help us orient ourselves within this terri-
tory, to fashion a map through the plays as a map of the night sky can
help seafarers navigate the oceans.

SIGHTS AND SOUNDS

If you're familiar with Wright's poetry, then you know that he draws
from many sources in addition to the Dogon, Bamana, and other
African cultures. If you aren't familiar with Wright's poetry, then this
fact is a good place from which to start encountering these plays.

Wright's palette is multicolored. Ogotemmêli will share a stanza with
Spanish Modernist poets, physicist and early contributor to quantum
theory Niels Bohr, presocratic Greek philosophers such as Heraclitus
and Anaximander, and more, each a face on a multifaceted geometric
object of Wright's design. For example, pore over this verse from *The
Prime Anniversary* (2019):

> In Pittsburgh, no Victorian ever suffers
> a tropospheric complacency, or gets caught
> in ice—always careful to avoid the vespers
> of a mere "form of words." They say that Frege bought
> a paradox that left him without a true soul
> and exposed to the phased molecule of logic.
> Why should those in Mali believe in the systole
> and diastole of vernacular too caustic
> as a testable state of affairs? We measure
> demand for existence without hope of a cure.[11]

11 *Prime Anniversary*, 9.

Or this one from *Thirteen Quintets for Lois* (2021):

> You flow within this densely ordered space,
> in search of reason's lost coherent sign—
> Lockean substance dancing with its law.
> *Già ogni stella cade*, not one trace
> and altered state that will show a design.
> Gondenu: day of dancing without flaw.[12]

Matthew Goulish and I mapped the expanse of Wright's references in *Pitch and Revelation*, and for those interested in Wright's poetry, I recommend visiting that volume.[13]

The plays, as with the poetry, are complex tapestries of thought, emotion, and philosophy. It is not my intention to offer an exhaustive reading of the plays here. Instead, along with the other essays in this book, I'd like to offer a few select sounds from these sights, which is to say, forays and highlight-hitting tours through the theatrical landscape that Wright has created. Like the poetry, these plays sing. As theater, the texts fashion seeing places to which we can arrive and glimpse microcosms of the world's many realities. Thus, sights and sounds are blended into a synesthetic experience that plays on the nervous system to produce an unforgettable sensation, something like that feeling that remains after having visited the Grand Canyon or Teotihuacán. The vastness of the scenes merges with the rebound of your voice's echo to fashion and imprint a memory the light of which may dim but never disappear.

The method here is, then, part dramaturgical, part analytical, and part philosophical. The aim is neither to explain the plays nor unpack each of the symbols collected in their pages but, rather, to offer up some sounds from these sights, some leading tones that can prepare

12 Wright, *Thirteen Quintets for Lois* (Chicago: Flood Editions, 2021), 9.
13 Will Daddario and Matthew Goulish, *Pitch and Revelation: Reconfigurations of Poetry, Philosophy, and Reading through the Work of Jay Wright* (Santa Barbara, CA: Punctum Books, 2022).

readers, performers, and artistic teams alike for a complete staging. After all, as plays, these texts require bodies to turn them all the way on.

THE SOUL ON TRIAL

Wright's plays have the feel of ritual about them, but what kind of ritual? What purpose do the rituals serve? A line delivered by Muso in Wright's play *Aria* hints at an answer:

> Imagine a theatre shorn of its ankle bells. Imagine its flamboyant solidity, its egregious color. What would you then have? Why, a perfect home to put the spirit on trial.[14]

This statement provides insight into many of Wright's plays from vols. 1 and 2. He frequently drops us into a purposefully rendered yet ecologically ambiguous, void-like setting where we find an ensemble of characters seeking some kind of resolution. *Aria* certainly fits that scenario, as do *Lemma*, *The Playing Space*, and *Syntax*. We might, therefore, keeping Muso's words in our ears, read these bands of characters as figures undergoing a trial. Their wanderings are not aimless. The characters are, to the contrary, in passage to some new state, one that maintains connection to the memories of Earthly existence but also partakes more purely in the spiritual dimension of rhythm, number, time, and space. But does this trial remind us of any particular cosmology?

Ancient Egypt comes to mind. And Wright has brought us to Egypt before, specifically in his poetic works. I would go as far as to say that the collected volume *Transfigurations* presents Wright's poetry as, overall, a ritual incantation that serves to prepare the body for passage from one world into the next. Jan Assmann's *Death and Salvation in Ancient Egypt* (2005) reveals the historical context of this keyword, transfiguration. Writing on the funeral rites that accompanied the embalming of Ancient Egyptians, he argues,

> But far more important than the surgical intervention and chemical treatment was the verbal treatment of the deceased. The inscriptions

14 Wright, *Selected Plays*, vol. 1, 362.

cited above [taken from hieroglyphs examined by the author] summarize this aspect of the embalming with the phrase "transfiguration by the lector priest." The lector priest—literally translated, the Egyptian title means "he who carries the book-roll"—accompanied the activities of the embalmers with the recitation of mortuary liturgies that he read from a roll of papyrus. This merging of action and speech, and specifically, speech set down in writing, is entirely characteristic of the Egyptian mortuary cult. [...] In the Egyptian language, this "talking therapy" for the dead is designated by an essentially untranslatable word that is rendered in English and French as "transfiguration" and in German as *Verklärung*. In this treatment, the deceased is constantly talked to. This stream of speech apparently had the function of a connective medium that was deployed, in connection with rituals and amulets, as a means of endowing with life. The deceased thus became a being endowed with consciousness and physical strength, capable of returning to life in a number of forms.[15]

Keeping the Dogon historiography in mind, we might also read Wright's poetry collected in *Transfigurations* as a version of this "stream of speech" serving to endow the dead with a vital force capable of venturing boldly into the afterlife.

If Wright's poetry reads as transfiguration—in this sense of the word—then perhaps a few of his selected plays bring us to the next stage, the trial of the dead on the cusp of the afterlife. In the Ancient Egyptian tradition, *akh* was the word given to the transfigured soul of the dead person that survived physical death. If judged to be deserving by Maat, the goddess of Truth, Justice and Balance, then the *akh* would live on in the next world while retaining the ability to influence states of affairs in the terrestrial realm. Perhaps, then, we can understand Muso's words in *Aria* as a kind of place marker, one that denotes the playing spaces of Wright's theater as located in the

15 Jan Assmann, *Death and Salvation in Ancient Egypt*, trans. David Lorton (Ithaca, NY: Cornell University Press, 2005), 33.

in-between stage after the death of the mortal being and before the final judgment of Maat. Even if this location is not literally accurate or cannot be applied to the totality of Wright's plays (and surely it can't and shouldn't be), it is nonetheless helpful to think of Wright's plays unfolding in a place where the stakes are exactly this high. The plays pass a verdict on the souls of the characters gathered. Even when comedic, the plays have a seriousness to them that correspond(s) to the trial being undertaken.

Esteban Rodríguez's essay in this volume raises this question about Wright's theater and the soul's trial through a discussion of purgatory. "For readers of Jay Wright's poetry," he suggests, "there might be a sense of entering a purgatorial space the moment they dive into the page." That is, readers enter "a particular type of limbo, one more colloquial than doctrinal, and there is always a distinct possibility that at the end of a poem, questions will be much more abundant than answers." Rodríguez goes on to say that audience members might find themselves entering a similar space when confronted with the plays, especially in the case of Wright's multi-part work *The Delights of Memory*. That play's matriarchal character, Lily Porter, is, according to Rodríguez, fully engaged in producing a reckoning for her family members, one in which their souls face their lives' sins. The play's action, then, especially its final part titled "Awaking and Forgetting," is a dramatization of Muso's provocation. Audiences watch the soul go on trial and the play's action swirls around the question of redemption. Is redemption attainable? Is there an exit to the purgatory of Mesa City, the fictional town in which the play takes place? Questions will be much more abundant than answers.

This theme of the soul on trial shows up in seemingly naturalistic plays like *The Delights of Memory* (though, as I'll explain later, this "naturalism" is an intriguing problem in its own right) as well as in the more abstract plays. Consider *The Playing Space*. In this work, Wright introduces us to an ensemble of entangled individuals. Brando, Kala, Grus, and Gaudentius appear in the eponymous playing space, a kind of coeval theater that yokes together the worksite of the actors playing the characters and the fictional realm of the play's drama. The playing space, then, refers to, or doubles as, the theater's black box and also something like a purgatorial place of trial, one dotted with altars that portend a grand, ritualistic transformation.

Actors and characters collaborate in discovering the ideal configuration of their bodies in this space. Gaudentius offers an apt meta-theatrical comment:

> Somewhere along the line, engaged in our joyous and enlightening narratives, we moved, that is to say, with respect to each other—that is, with respect to the altars' relationship with each other—we reorganized, reordered, however you want to put it, our spatial configuration by which we had oriented ourselves before, that is, before this new relationship became operative.[16]

One of Wright's great skills is his ability to draw our attention to the live moment of the performance's offing. We imagine that the actors' labors, their skill at speaking words in the most effective register and arranging themselves artfully within this theatrical space, will somehow help the characters find the remedy they are searching for. We are never quite sure what this remedy is, however, and that fact brings the audience into purgatory with the players. We are all waiting upon some kind of salvation, one that hinges on the correct use of the multidimensional playing space.

In the case of this play, the issue seems to be one of re-presentation. Finding themselves in this site where their collective soul is on trial, the characters rehearse words and actions that they performed in their previous lives. They believe, and perhaps this is their mistake, that they are working to be reborn into their previous existence:

> KALA: Then we can retrieve the situation by going back to the status quo ante?
>
> GAUDENTIUS: Exactly.[17]

16 Wright, *Selected Plays*, vol. 1, 157–158.
17 *Selected Plays*, vol. 1, 158.

But what work is required to facilitate this return? Is it even possible to return to one's life? Grus is skeptical:

> Think about it. What would we have to do to assure ourselves that we had come back to our place, reconfigured the proper relationships, if you will? We'd have to go over the same ground, tell the same stories, get into the same quarrels, talk about the same proposals, visions, dreams.[18]

It seems as if Wright is formulating a question. When we come to the great theater that awaits us after we die, the playing space in which, we hope, our best performance will carry us into the next life, are we aiming to return to our former selves or venture off in a new direction? This theater may be the place where the spirit goes on trial, but what is the verdict we are seeking? Are we aiming to be reborn or recast in a new form?

WHO ARE THESE FOLKS?

One way that Wright builds our stamina to tarry with such philosophical questions is through his artful figurations and characterizations. Each of the figures who grace these playing spaces has a distinct allure and charm linked to his or her way of speaking, moving, thinking. Even before they utter a word, the characters perform through their names, which alight on the page with all the polysemous power we've come to expect from Wright's poetry. Take, for example, the family name of the characters we meet in *The Delights of Memory*: the Porters. That name, common enough, begins to unload its freight when we recall that *portar* is the verb for "to carry." We know these characters are carrying a great weight, as is evidenced by the details Wright writes into their feet:

> [Lily] *Her shoes are cut near the big and little toes to ease her feet.*[19]

> [Doss] *He is a tall skeleton of jangling bones. His walk is a punch-drunk fighter's lurch on painful feet. He wears [. . .] a pair of crackling leather shoes, out of which he has cut the areas around his big toes to ease his bunions.*[20]

---

18 *Selected Plays*, vol. 1, 158.

19 *Selected Plays*, vol. 2, 225.

20 *Selected Plays*, vol. 2, 251.

Leroy is introduced alongside his "pair of scuffed brown shoes" and "torn socks."[21] In fact, the first several actions underpinning Leroy's speech are related to the struggle of putting on shoes.

These details, paired with the name Porter, help us map the dramaturgy of the play, which, perhaps, leads toward a consideration of the characters' burdens and the means by which they will displace, discard, or disentangle from those burdens.

But sometimes, due to Wright's metatheatrical sensibilities, the playwright forces us to question our mode of dramaturgical analysis. In *Lemma*, for example, Wright offers us a dizzying array of names. Each character seems to have at least two names, or, if two names aren't affixed outright, the character will perform multiple roles throughout the play's action. *Lemma* starts with a suite of voices from Voice A to Voice F. We eventually find that these voices have names: Tibio, Lorg, Bricco, Bacán, Spalla, and Polso. But then these characters also go by other names: Tibio is also Fuadach, Bricco is at one time referred to as John, Spalla and Bacán each acts out the memories of two figures called Elzbieta and Carmen, Lorg doubles as Ginocchio, and Polso as Giuig. Sometimes the characters wear masks, too, which adds another layer of identity to the mix. Clearly something is going on here, but we can't simply say that the names mean x because Polso/Giuig demands, "I said call me Polso. The names mean nothing."[22]

We can take Polso at his word and also deconstruct the character's statement. The names may "mean" nothing, and yet they certainly *produce* a rich intertextual web of connotation. Polso, Ginocchio, Spalla. These words translate, from Italian into English, as Wrist, Knee, and Shoulder. If we turn Tibio's name to the feminine—Tibia—then we have another bone, that part of the lower leg that pairs with the Fibula. Arranged in this way, the characters' names reveal not individual characters but, perhaps, individual parts of a single body. Building on the dramaturgy of Ancient Egyptian funeral practices mentioned earlier,

21 Wright, *Selected Plays*, vol. 2, 273.
22 *Selected Plays*, vol. 1, 191.

might we see in *Lemma* an attempt to "pull oneself together" once one has crossed over from the land of the living? The characters attempt to find the perfect arrangement among themselves—"I like this new configuration," says Spalla early on, for example—as if assembling a broken body into the semblance of a whole.

But this isn't *the* key to unlocking the dramaturgy of *Lemma*'s names. We have already heard from one character that the names "mean" nothing. In *The Possible Impossibility of Leaving Home*,[23] another character, Filo, castigates a Boy for being "A fucking little nominalist." Add to this the significance of polysemy in Wright's poetry, and, clearly, we receive enough warning to steer clear of overly simple arithmetic equations in our dramatic analysis. Look, for example, at the way Wright not only presents names with specific meanings rendered through linguistic translation but also names that unite seemingly disparate cultures.

Tibio translates to "warm" or "tepid." Sure, maybe we receive some instruction on the character's temperament here. We also hear the feminine, tibia, and develop a picture of a shin bone, perhaps one seeking connection with other bones. Tibio, however, is also Fuadach, a word that refers to "kidnapping" or "abduction" in Gaelic. And we could glom onto that word's connection to either the play's theme of the fugitivity of memory or the partial recollection, expressed by Fuadach, of taking a former lover, Elzbieta, away from her town. Again, though, the exact equation (name $= x$) is less interesting than the merger of Gaelic and Spanish or Latin cultures. The body of Tibio/Fuadach is the meeting point between a Spanish and a Gaelic name. Similarly, the body of Ginocchio/Lorg is a meeting of Italian (another Romance language) and Gaelic. As a verb, "Lorg," in Gaelic, means "to seek" or "to find." As a noun it means "mark" or "trace," as in a trace that has been left as evidence. On one level, Lorg is the remedy to Fuadach's kidnapping. On another level, Wright has given us two characters that fuse two geographically distinct cultures. Three, in fact, since Polso is also Giuig, a "witch" in Scottish Gaelic. Wright's work

---

23 *Selected Plays*, vol. 2, 413.

here with the names, then, reminds us that, while geographically and ethnically distinct, Gaelic and Spanish peoples have a common point of origin. The Gaelic people seem to have originated in the Spanish province of Galicia.

What is Wright up to? As I show in my other essay in this volume, *Lemma* contains numerous direct citations to texts by Robert Graves, Luke the Evangelist, E.M. Forster, Elizabeth Anscombe, John Donne, and Nicolas of Cusa. Like the multiple body parts seeking the proper configuration of a singular body, these multiple historic figures fit together like notes in a musical chord to produce a harmonic resonance between and across cultures. The harmony, or the fitting, between multiple parts: this is the primary sound tucked within the action of *Lemma*. Even the play's name urges this consideration. A lemma in the discourse of logic is a passage forged through a minor proposition en route to a decisive proof. In lexicography, a lemma is the "canonical form" from which issues a set of related words (e.g., dance: dance, dances, danced, dancing). Psycholinguists use "lemma" to name the abstract concept of a word that the brain selects prior to uttering anything, a kind of mental model from which will sprout a sound laden with meaning. With Wright's play, we find a new valence to "lemma." The text is a transition point, a hinge, or perhaps a port of embarkation that doubles as a cellular matrix from which grows both potential and actual lives (which always contain pasts, presents, and futures). Lemma takes place at the horizon where a memory is given form through the precise language and musicality with which that memory is spoken.

One take-away from this realization is that, while the names of the characters may, as Polso says, mean nothing, the sounds of the names tune our ears to Wright's signature polysemic blends, the way in which his work harmonizes notes or ideas or themes or styles that may, on first appraisal, seem dissonant to one another. Whether we are working through *Lemma* or any of Wright's plays collected in *The Dramatic Radiance of Number* and *Figurations and Dedications*, we are dealing with dramatic literature and theatricality that speaks of mixture.

Given the importance of mixture and polysemy in Wright's work, it will come as no surprise that these plays reside outwith genre. That is, we paint ourselves into corners if we approach any of the titles as tragedies or comedies or farces. Umbrella terms like "naturalist" or "realist" or "experimental" (in its overly vague and commodified contemporary usage) will also fail to ignite the powder kegs of affect planted within each text. If we borrow from French and US art history, where the term "genre paintings" denoted artworks that capture scenes from everyday life, we likewise run into dead-ends, both because Wright's dramatic landscapes frequently unfold from other-worldly, sacred sites unbeholden to the Euclidean laws structuring "everyday life" and also because the stillness of painted scenes clashes directly with the vivacious rhythms of Wright's characters' speech and behaviors. We could try, one more time, to find something spicier in the realm of music, such that *The Disappearance of Mexico* becomes intelligible neither as comedy nor farce but, rather, as *corrido* or *tejano* or *norteño*. But even then the play would be *typed* and, by extension, rendered within a discernable generic *topos* that blunts the artistic improvisation and surprising cross-pollination that makes these plays Wright-eous.

Consider, too, the genre/topos of "Black." Could we, should we, ought we understand and approach Wright's plays as expressions emanating from the wider (generic/genetic) family of Black Theater in the United States? If we assent, then we quickly come face to face with the established timeline of African-American and Black US theater such that Wright's plays are made to share some genetic material with Angelina W. Grimké's *Rachel*, the various offerings of the Ethiopian Art Theatre, the Negro Playwrights' Company, and the Black Arts Repertory Theatre. We'd have to fit Wright into this groove somehow, making sure to account equally for his affinity to and resistance against both the Harlem Renaissance and the Black Arts Movement. In this light, maybe Wright has a stronger affinity with Adrienne Kennedy, both in terms of the long duration of their artistic output (i.e., work that spans decades) and their tendency to unite autobiography with experimental theatricality. But if, say, Wright and Kennedy make up an intriguing ticket, or Wright and Suzan-Lori Parks for that matter, does a pairing like that firmly establish Wright as a Black playwright? Or does the whole line of questioning return to his *being* Black?

It's not the case that these questions and equations aren't interesting or even important for the development of dramaturgical dossiers on Wright's selected plays; rather, the problem is that identifying Wright's genre serves, ultimately, only to limit the range of interpretations that artistic teams might bring to his work. If we think of Wright's plays as musical scores—which makes sense given the musicality of his broader poetic output as well as his self-identification as a *musica latina* bassist—then our primary question ceases to be "What genre is this?" and becomes "How do we play this thing?" And, again, we could make the mistake of dragging genre into the picture, as in, "Oh, it's jazz. We play it like jazz." Well OK, but is it Art Tatum or John Zorn? Or are we looking at something like an imagined love child between the two with an active recessive Cuban *son* gene in there? Ultimately, my argument is to leave genre aside and listen to the way that the texts tactically baffle most generic standards. To stage these plays, and even to read them silently to ourselves, we benefit from playing among and between recognizable forms in order to conjure theatrical worlds much in the same way that ritual acts conjure portals between the sacred and the profane. Playing in this way will unmoor us from inflexible binds to "jazz aesthetics," "Black theater," "theatrical naturalism," or "realism" and, instead, lead us into other territories.

We could consider *Homage to Anthony Braxton* with all this in mind. The title of the play alone forces us to make some decisions. As an "homage," are we supposed to look for Braxton—the endlessly inventive composer, musician, native Chicagoan, early member of the Association for the Advancement of Creative Musicians—in between the words on the page? If so, how do we understand Braxton's work? Is it jazz or not jazz? Is it political or apolitical? Is it Black? What's Black about it? What's left out from consideration if we let those questions shape our listening experience? Ultimately, in line with the argument I spooled out in the previous paragraphs, the questions raised by the title lead us off on quite a journey, one that finds a parallel quest in the journey launched through each of the other plays gathered in *Selected Plays* vols. 1 and 2. The purpose for going on the trip is to find our way out beyond the confines of generic classification and into some new territory whose topography could be laid bare through live staging.

In this present volume, two authors take up the challenge of *Braxton*. David Grubbs and Devin King map a good swath of dramaturgical territory for us to explore. As Grubbs says plainly, "It's not immediately clear what about this work nominates it as an homage to the composer and musician Anthony Braxton." Sensing a similar quandary, King probes the meta-structure of the play and ends up turning toward Braxton's own writings, specifically his discussion of the "dramatic under-sense" of narrative from the composer-philosopher's essay "Narrative Structures."[24] King interprets this phrase as "a lack of a final dramatic context that focuses the audience-member into what might be called catharsis." In other words, not only does the title of Wright's play leave more questions than answers, and not only does the play's action stop short of providing audiences with the satisfaction of a meaning-full "ah-ha!" moment, but Wright, following Braxton's tune, also challenges the need for tidy knot work in the denouement and embraces, instead, a kind of synesthetic gestalt. As King's essay concludes, "Wright and Braxton create a narrative—a dramatic—playing field where the audience member is asked, with some slight level of improvisational freedom given focus by the structure of Braxton's scores or Wright's narratives, in Wright's words, 'to accept the poem's challenge and to listen to, walk along, sing along and be with the poem. To play in, to walk along.'"[25]

24 Braxton, "Narrative Structures," *Anthony Braxton Research Papers*, https://tricentricfoundation.org/anthony-braxton-narrative-structures.
25 Charles H. Rowell, "'The Unraveling of the Egg': An Interview with Jay Wright," in "Jay Wright: A Special Issue," *Callaloo* 19 (Autumn 1983): 7.

Grubbs and King both approach *Braxton* by walking through its plot. Hank and Annie, the two characters we meet first, draw our attention throughout the play even though they also exist as nodes within an equally central and vast network of activity. As Grubbs puts it, "The play orbits around the two of them, a dyad of hustlers immemorial." We watch these two, and all the other characters/nodes, play out a quotidian iteration of their general lifescript in a place called Freedom Park. As Grubbs also notes, all character activity intersects with an impending rally for one Pastor Benjamin Ames, which is to take place in this park, upon a stage that reminds audience members attending *Braxton* that there's a metatheatrical commentary here, a stage within a stage. We might actually spy a nested series of stages: the under-construction set for the Ames rally within the park, which is itself one performance space (housing performances of everyday life) within the broader unnamed city serving as the setting of this play, within the theater housing *Homage to Anthony Braxton* (wherever that may end up being).

The ebb and flow of the action produces waves of tension and release that help audience members to glimpse strategic alliances between the characters as well as hard and fast obstacles that prevent certain intimacies from ever forming. For example, we meet Johnny Walker, "a black man in his middle twenties, short, vigorous" whose authentic Blackness is questioned by two unnamed male characters. Thus, even though Wright specifies an all Black cast in the character descriptions that start the text, audiences watch any semblance of a monolithic Blackness fall away to reveal a molecular heterogeneity of Black identity. Dialectically, however, Wright prompts Hank to preach on several occasions about the challenges faced by simply being Black, thereby bringing the monolith of Blackness back into the spotlight. Hank and Johnny appear to form a bond at one point, thus fashioning the dialectical tension of Blackness's minimal difference into a salient narrative or dramaturgical theme. But that budding relationship gets snipped at the play's conclusion when shots are fired and the action of *Braxton* comes to a crashing halt.

What's going on here? For starters, Grubbs's and King's arguments and approaches to the play are both compelling and highly defensible. Each one riffs, one more explicitly than the other, on the notion of "restructuralism" and offers an invitation to dig into the biographical intersections between the play's characters and both Braxton and Wright. Please do spend time with those two contributions in this volume. They help us, in other words, keep an eye on the elusive figure of Anthony Braxton within the story of Hank and Annie and Johnny Walker and Pastor Ames.

My interest, however, is in the move from page to stage that artistic companies will take when they opt to produce *Braxton*. Lest a few of the text's most noticeable signifiers overshadow the dramaturgical approach to the play—for example, the all Black cast, the "urban" setting, the slang slung by the highly verbal characters—I'd like to continue my advocacy for leaving genre behind and especially for avoiding the trap of presenting the play as an example of realism, naturalism, Black naturalism, or as an opportunity to build on the contemporary discourse of multiculturalism. What I sense, instead, is that such generic classifications would not only oversimplify the mode of theater Wright imagines through his texts, but, more importantly, would ignore Wright's ability to recast generic categories into new mixtures that require the kind of listening compelled not only by jazz, which certainly provides useful interpretive strategies where Wright is concerned, but also by trans-disciplinary music such as that created by Anthony Braxton. When we see a play like *Braxton*, draped as it is in recognizable features of Black, urban identity, we can also listen to and perceive its recognizable features as elements of a *détournement* that point the way to alternate visionings of and engagements with cultural identity.

My argument took shape through an email exchange with contemporary playwright Caridad Svich. I had reached out to her in order to seek advice on the topic of "high language" (Where does that term come from? Is it still relevant? What are the power dynamics smuggled into the phrase?) from someone much more connected to and knowledgeable of the emergent front of dramatic poetry in today's theater landscape than I. I was specifically concerned that artistic teams encountering plays like *Braxton* might too swiftly assess Wright's language as *either* "high" *or* "low." Siding with the former, I imagined, would place Wright's text into the category of "unintelligible" or, worse, "elitist." Siding with the latter, by distinction, would place the text into readymade categories such as "urban" or "street" or "multicultural." More accurately, I believe, the text baffles the binaries of High and Low, Black and White, Street and Salon, Poetry and Prose, Multicultural and, what would it be, Hegemonic? Mainstream? Whatever is happening in *Braxton* isn't something we should bind with binary thinking.

To test your ears, consider the opening lines from *Braxton* between Hank and Annie:

HANK: Annie, if times get any harder in this nappy swamp, a lean dog will have to sew his tail to his booty to keep from quiverin' to death. I can't get my hand in nobody's pocket. [*Twisting his hand around.*] Yes, sir, I gave up labor for management. Takin' all money in trust. [*Pushing his hands in his pockets.*] I want some action. I'd as soon play with a nickel as play with a dollar.

ANNIE: Well, I been doin' good.

HANK: I know you have. I been askin' you why we don't run together. I got a stone new hustle ought to skin a three-fanged rattler.

ANNIE: Baby, your drawers ain't slick and your brog*ans* is too blunt. Besides that, you get too loud in the bars when I got my hand on one of them dap motor scooters from the west side.

HANK: I can't stand them flea hoppin' jigs who done scratched they way out the Bottom. He's doin' good, and damn you. But he always come back to the Bottom for his ballin'.

ANNIE: They ain't all okey doke and no smoke, Hank. Some of 'em got a definite strong feelin' for the people.[26]

26 Wright, *Selected Plays*, vol. 2, 89–90.

Svich confirmed for me that my worries were valid: "as you point out—intellectual vs popular, difficult vs accessible, poetic vs prose—are sadly very much binaries that are still with us. accessible associated with 'common' (i.e. low) and difficult associated with 'elitist, narrow, cerebral.' i will say this is mostly true still in US theater. the strain of anti-intellectualism in the US runs deep."[27] I had suggested that, to elude binary thinking, I wanted to think of Wright's plays—and passages like the one above in particular—in terms of register and tuning. What are the notes of his "scales," so to speak? What kind of "vocal training" is required to "sing" in the register that Wright writes? And Svich, again, provided helpful insight:

> its certainly true of how i think about my own work—as functioning/operating in keys. poetic vein. sung-speech. with hybridity of linguistic and sonic registers, amplified and acoustic storytelling/sound-telling (as I call it. my term!), the musicality of sequencing, repetition and patterning to convey kinesthetic meaning and affect. the intellect is involved, of course, but i don't separate the cerebral from the visceral.

All of which brought us back around to the persistent—though maybe gradually diminishing?—equations that claim "poetic" language = "difficult" language = (acceptable in the form of) White Classics, and, at the same time, "street" language = "real-er" language = multicultural (read "Black") texts.

The problem with staging Wright's plays is that neither line of thought is applicable. *Braxton* and the other plays are poetic songs woven from observations made during sojourns through many streets across the world and insights hewn from deep study of mytho-histories galore. Though they come from a recognizably (phenotypically) Black writer who cut his playwriting teeth during the Black Arts Movement, they are not immediately amenable to many of the readymade dramaturgical templates often applied to plays by other Black playwrights. Again the question becomes: how are we supposed to play these things?

27 This and all quotations of Svich come from an email correspondence with the author.

One possible answer to that question comes from a close reading of an article by René V. Arcilla called "Abstract Art as Alternative to Multicultural Education." The most urgent of Arcilla's desires is that we challenge the tendency to deepen our understanding of the multicultural world by studying works of art that clearly represent the explicitly, say, Black contexts from which those works emerge. The act of spotlighting works of art that offer seemingly concrete representations of, in this case, Black society, such as the thriving Harlem neighborhood of the 1940s, too often comes hand in hand with an active ignoring of abstract art, the form and content of which frequently provides no direct line of sight into culturally-specific modes of being.

Arcilla's example of this is Norman Lewis's painting *Phantasy II*, which, due to its abstract nature, is likely not as useful to teachers of multicultural humanities classes because of its perceived affinity to the predominantly White abstract expressionist art movement of the time. Such a painting doesn't appear to document the lived reality of African-Americans living in Harlem in the 1940s, despite the fact that Lewis was an African-American man from a proletarian background. Arcilla admits that, "if we are primarily interested in cultural understanding as such, it makes sense in general to favor the study of other kinds of works. Historical documents and scientific, philosophical, critical, and artistic works that comment directly on cultural history are more valuable for this multiculturalist teacher and her students."[28] The shortcoming of that approach, however, is that it "demotes artistic, imaginative works to second-class status in humanities teaching."[29]

The problem is twofold. First, by looking past abstract works of art and favoring those works that directly represent and more clearly emerge from historical events and structures particular to cultures whose modes of being are typically overwritten by dominant (White) culture, teachers end up reifying cultural identities into recognizable forms.

---

28 René V. Arcilla, "Abstract Art as Alternative to Multiculturalist Education," *Philosophy of Education* (2009): 218.

29 Arcilla, 219.

These forms solidify through repeat teaching, while, in turn, the becoming of identity drops out of the conversation. In Arcilla's words, "Abstract art, in short, invites us to delight in the transformation of contingent forms that a medium engenders—'delight' because the product suggests a new feeling rather than represents an old one."[30] Second, then, when more useful and recognizably "African-American" or "Black" works of art replace abstract works in pedagogical settings, it is possible that students overlook the joy of transformation. Transformation, change, movement, and instability: these qualities destabilize our assumptions of certainty that frequently underwrite our identification of certain works of art as, say, Black and/or Multicultural. The dynamism of culture slows to a halt and the life of emergent identities becomes artificially stabilized for scrutiny in the classroom (or the theater).

Anthony Braxton's work helps us link Arcilla to Wright. Arcilla cites Braxton's music as an illuminating example of abstraction, particularly his Charlie Parker Project. While *Bongo Bop* is a fitting piece to grapple with, I think *Ornithology* may be a better piece for this discussion of *Braxton*. In that work, Braxton reworks the classic Parker tune of the same name and adds a face-melting contrabass saxophone solo that, as Stuart Broomer says, seems to convert musical pitch into a haptic reckoning with our established sense of time. Writing on the "marked emphasis on extremely low frequencies in Anthony Braxton's music," Broomer explains that

> The lower the range, the more we struggle to identify notes and their relationships. Listening becomes akin to ear training, as we make distinctions between bass frequencies usually reserved for players of extremely low-pitched instruments. We stretch to hear because we are operating at the limits of our hearing and the beginning of inaudibility. Pitches become ambiguous, as the lower a note on a tuba or contra-bass clarinet is, the more it vacillates between pitches.[31]

30 Arcilla, 221.

31 Stuart Broomer, "Pitch into Time: Notes on Anthony Braxton's Lower Register," *Critical Studies in Improvisation* 4.1 (2008): 73.

As we listen to Braxton's *Ornithology*, our ears (in step with the totality of our proprioceptive and interoceptive sense awareness) dive down to follow the pitch of the contrabass sax. Eventually, our ears "reach oscillations that can be heard as time, not pitch. Thus the C six octaves below middle C might be described as a metronome rhythm of 240 beats per minute. We have thus used the same measurement to move from a description of pitch to a description of time."[32]

Arcilla might say that Braxton's "abstract" rendering of *Ornithology* presents a wonderful pedagogical opportunity for students of the humanities. I would agree while also adding that "abstract" becomes a rather useless adjective once we analyze all that *Ornithology* clearly puts forth. On the surface level, we have one Black musician (Braxton) repeating (with revision) a classic tune constructed by another Black musician (Parker) who had, likewise, built the chord progression of his song on an earlier tune (*How High the Moon*, by Morgan Lewis), thereby offering students a material manifestation of what playwright Suzan-Lori Parks calls "rep and rev," repetition and revision, a particularly meaningful artistic strategy utilized by Black US artists to infuse hallmarks of dominant culture with precisely that (in this case Blackness) which was so often excluded from dominant culture. Moving one level deeper, into the territory where the contrabass sax roams, we have a temporal commentary. As our ears slip from pitch into time, we might wonder how the image of Parker has been transformed through its historical uses and abuses. We might ponder, for example, how his status as musical genius came to overshadow the sound of struggle—linked to racist nationalism—in his life and work, or how, lauded by Beat poets like Jack Kerouac, his music motivated a form of jazz- and bebop-inspired literature that still commands critical applause today for its status as a quintessentially (White) American writing style. But what of Parker's life as a Black man? Has Parker's Blackness faded from our ears? To what type of knowledge do we gain access by asking questions like this? What other questions might we ask? Are the questions contained in the form and content of the music, or do we,

32 Broomer, 73.

the listener, invent them ourselves? And, finally, down into a still yet deeper level, if we read these questions next to Braxton's own reception, what kind of arguments can we make about the contortions Black musicians need to make to enter into the canon? As Grubbs mentions in his essay in this volume, and as many other writers have noted, Braxton is frequently challenged as somehow not aligned *enough* or *well enough* with the proper (read "Black") Blues tradition. *Ornithology* presents all three layers of discussion for students because of, not in spite of, its blend of musical standard with musical innovation. Arcilla wants more of this in the classroom, and "this" is material, concrete, right there in the form of the music, which is to say more than abstract.

Technically speaking,[33] Braxton's *Ornithology* is a musical contrafact: "In jazz, a melody built upon the chord progression of another piece (after *contrafactum*, in medieval and Renaissance music)." Adding that terminology to the flight of thought made possible by Arcilla's essay, I argue that we should listen to *Homage to Anthony Braxton* as a contrafact, too, where contrafact defines not a genre but an artistic tactic. *Braxton* is a contrafact of Black, Urban theater, which is itself a rep and rev production sparked by the intricate materiality of Black lives, which is itself a dynamic brew of ideas, gestures, speech, and physicality woven into the great weave of the world. The "chord progression" on which Wright models his composition may indeed be the hustle and economics perfected by Black people who find themselves at the margins of dominant culture, forced by specific political forces to live, like Hank and Annie and Johnnie Walker, in parks or other urban heterotopias. In lieu of a contrabass solo, Wright infuses those chords with his language, verses that baffle the high/low language binary and

---

33 Grove Music Online, s.v. "Contrafact," https://doi.org/10.1093/gmo/9781561592630.article.J543100. See also s.v. "Forms": "At other times the connection is based on insider's information: the title *Ornithology* (the study of birds) does not refer to its chordal source (*How High the Moon*) but to its opening phrase, a lick that Charlie Parker (whose nickname was Bird) often used." (Grove Music Online, s.v. "Forms," by Thomas Owens, https://doi.org/10.1093/gmo/9781561592630.article.J154400.

rip through time-space with such velocity that our ears will need to come to the theater already warmed-up and ready to listen. If theater ensembles can learn to read *Homage to Anthony Braxton* as a contrafact of, say, canonical Black US dramatic poetry that frequently takes up themes of Black quotidian existence (instead of as an instance of that canonical theater), then they will be able to play it, despite the fact that it is scripted, with the *ad libitum* required to make manifest the innovative spirit of the text. In the end, does the play register as Black or as multicultural theater? The answer to that question will require us to deconstruct and rethink what precisely Black and multicultural might mean. *Homage to Anthony Braxton* extends an invitation to contemporary theater makers to pick up that task.

DEGREES OF PERSPECTIVE

All of Wright's plays gathered in the two volumes that precede the one you're reading now call us to deconstruct and rethink what precisely theater is and could be. The works challenge readers and spectators to engage critically in the act of representation so crucial to theatrical works of art. Here, however, "representation" has a specific meaning, one that Henri Bergson parses in *Matter and Memory* (1896):

> Our representation of matter is the measure of our possible action upon bodies: it results from the discarding of what has no interest for our needs, or more generally for our functions. In one sense we might say that the perception of any unconscious material point whatever, in its instantaneousness, is infinitely greater and more complete than ours, since this point gathers and transmits the influences of all the points of the material universe, whereas our consciousness only attains to certain parts and to certain aspects of those parts. Consciousness—in regard to external perception—lies in just this choice. But there is, in this necessary poverty of our conscious perception, something that is positive, that foretells spirit: it is, in the etymological sense of the word, discernment.[34]

34 Henri Bergson, *Matter and Memory*, trans. Nancy Margaret Paul and W. Scott Palmer (New York: Macmillan, 1919), 30–31.

On one level, Bergson is analyzing the slippage between the physi-
ology of our perception of matter, on the one hand, and the totality
of the matter we perceive, on the other. That totality exceeds the per-
ception we receive of a given substance because our act of perception
is always sutured to the use of that perception. The surplus of any
given "body" is rendered useless if it has no direct bearing on the
action we plan to take with the body we are perceiving. To be useless
is to be unperceived. On another level, though, something more is
happening. Consciousness in regard to our external perception, i.e.,
the act of choosing what aspect of a given totality may be most useful
for our needs in a given instant, touches upon the greater mysteries
of the universe precisely where it fails adequately to represent the
totality of those mysteries to the mind. While conscious perception
discerns the useful from among the whole, it also, through that same
discernment, grapples in some way with the functionally useless parts,
which is to say the spiritual dimension. This grappling is, in fact, the
spirituality of perception, and it always runs in the background like an
invisible program that touches the mysteries of the world but remains
silent about the findings from that touch. The word "discernment" is
key here because of its theatrical resonance. Discernment is akin to
enscenement, a theatrical production. The great theater of perception
encompasses the functional and the spiritual.

Similarly, Wright's plays raise our awareness of our Bergsonian
perceptual apparatuses. We watch the action he spools out before
us and we listen to the words uttered by the characters. In doing so,
we begin to piece together (render useful) the primary themes or
meanings of the plays: the spirit on trial, the entanglement of cultural
identities, the necessity of proper arrangement in the composition
of our life's actions. At the same time, however, beyond the realm
of useful meaning, there unfolds a spiritual fathoming. We don't so
much "do" this fathoming when we engage with the plays as we find
ourselves somehow always already integrated into the mysteries of that
spiritual dimension. What we walk away from the plays with—our
representation of their matter—function as footnotes to the greater

whole. Wright's theater both takes place in and as theater while also revealing the wider theatrical scene—discernment—of perception, the metatheatrical production in which we are always engaged.

Likewise, the "introduction" I'm offering here presents a useful representation of all that is going on with Wright's plays while at the same time it sounds the penumbra of the unseen—yet still perceived—whole. To add a few more degrees of vision to our conscious, functional perception, I'd like to prepare you for the other essays you'll encounter in vol. 3.

Earlier in this introduction, I referenced Esteban Rodríguez's essay in this volume dedicated to the multi-part play *The Delights of Memory* found in vol. 2 of *Selected Plays*. Michael Paul Berlin also approaches this text, but he provides a different angle on the figures and actions we find there. Whereas Rodríguez sensed a purgatorial theme running through the play's many parts, Berlin develops an argument about the impact of racial and societal trauma on the different generations of characters we encounter in the fictional town of Mesa, Arizona. Specifically, Berlin is interested in the interplay between silence and what must be said, pointing out that, "More than in his poetry, silence finds its measure against what must be said, but cannot yet be understood."

Daniel Woody's "The Radical Performance of Getting Lost: Multiplicity in Jay Wright's *The Possible Impossibility of Leaving Home*" guides us into the deep end of one of Wright's more challenging plays. The essay seems at first to proceed according to the plot or the story, as we saw in the works by Grubbs and King cited earlier, but soon takes a turn. Woody gets lost. Then, embracing the feeling of bewilderment that comes about during a first reading of the play, Woody tunes into an analogue experience from his own life during which he embraced a period of profound disillusionment and despair through purposeful acts of wandering throughout Chicago's city streets. He then summons the wisdom gained through those walks to orient himself within Wright's play where, with new eyes, he spies several vibrant threads composing the greater weave of *The Possible Impossibility of Leaving Home*. This analytical strategy helps map the play's literary and dramaturgical geography, including central figures and objects: Abiku, Mami Wata, an orchid. Along the way, he also bridges the literary world of the play's text with the potential theatrical worlds of the play's eventual staging. Woody offers us some powerful thoughts, such as this one:

> Since each character is a lost traveler, then there is space for each actor to interrogate their own realities, to perform rituals that are ancillary to the text, to devise sibling journeys, perhaps in rehearsal to deepen their embodiment of the role, or perhaps devised physical enactments of the tension between attachment and ascension.

The gift here comes in the form of an invitation for actors staging this (and other) play(s) to enrich their understanding of the ritual power of Wright's work through the enactment of their own rituals. This kind of paratheatrical potential stands out as one particular way in which Wright's text invite a new method of theater-making in this contemporary moment.

Sebastián Calderón Bentin's "Disappearance, Disappearing, Disappeared" focuses our attention elsewhere. He reminds us that, for all the density of prose, complex polysemy, theatrical ambiguity, and baffling of genre, Wright's texts touch upon specific political realities. For Calderón Bentin, the "death" limned through Wright's play *The Disappearance of Mexico* rhymes with Achille Mbembe's "death-worlds," "new and unique forms of social existence in which vast populations are subjected to living conditions that confer upon them the status of the living dead."[35] Mexico is not the only country to disappear in this way, Calderón Bentin reminds us. Though the point in this essay is not to draw a straight line between Wright's text and global necropolitics; rather, "Disappearance, Disappearing, Disappeared" invites us to immerse ourselves in the ambiguity of Wright's text, the way it calls to mind specific political realities as well as imaginative palimpsests of real and fictional landscapes. "In *The Disappearance of Mexico*,

---

35 Achille Mbembe, *Necropolitics* (Durham, NC: Duke U. Press, 2019), 92.

the words 'disappearance' and 'Mexico' begin a dance that moves between slipping and belonging, presence and disappearance, holding us in a space that only theater can create."

That is to say, we find ourselves in another one of Wright's Playing Spaces. This time, he introduces us to Gafo, Nono, Dusel, Dieb, and Falz. Their debates and exchanges lead to glimpses of a concrete plot and story—two companions encounter a trio of pilgrims who, paradoxically, resist the work of pilgrimage—but an audience can never be sure of where the horizon is. Calderón Bentin helps us navigate a journey through the text by marshaling the Portuguese word *saudade*, a place-based "admixture of mourning and gratitude," while carefully preserving the ambiguity or "slipperiness" of the play that marks it as one of Wright's creations.

Like Calderón Betin's chapter, my other essay in this collection, "*Lemma*: Jay Wright's Idiorrhythmic American Theater," helps place Wright within a specific historiographical network. This act of placing is, however, contingent on a necessary dis-placing, one that distances Wright from other playwrights of the Black Arts Movement with whom he is sometimes compelled to share space. To map the differences between BAM and Wright, I call upon Roland Barthes's term idiorrhythmy, which the French philosopher developed for his lectures at the Collège de France now published as *How to Live Together: Novelistic Simulations of Some Everyday Spaces* (2012). That term helps us read Wright's work as a kind of weaving that works to stitch together the Americas out of a radically heterogeneous combination of sources. In *Lemma*, these sources include indigenous reworkings of Christian cosmology, Robert Graves's mytho-history of Old Stone Age pantheons, the philosophy of Elizabeth Anscombe, John Donne's materiality, Nicolas of Cusa's mysticism, and a mode of music theory reminiscent of George Russell's *Lydian Chromatic Concept of Tonal Organization*. The point of unearthing these source materials within *Lemma* and attending to the musicality of the materials' arrangement within the dramatic text is to spy yet another type of work alive within Wright's plays, namely the work of a historiographer. As I write, for example, *Lemma* helps us find a "glimpse of the multitude that might thrive in all of us who identify as Americans if we broaden the scope of our identity to include practices and harmonies that have been occluded by dominant narratives of belonging."

Rather than explicitly explaining or analyzing the intertexts and performatives contained within and produced by Wright's dramatic literature, Duriel E. Harris has provided a creative response to vols. 1 and 2 of *Selected Plays* in the form of "a full-length play in progress" titled, *CODE: A Sport (Approaching Jay Wright)*. In the preface that precedes the text, she specifies that *Passage* and *Lemma* are the two plays that most directly influenced her contribution. The opening lines of *CODE* are delivered by Marlowe, "An ambitious undercover AI who appears in the form of a golden-eyed, dark brown furred, talking Maine coon domestic cat":

> [*in the style of soliloquy*] Words are the most powerful drug used by humankind? Meh. The idea of language as a "drug" and even the concept of the drug itself is passé. Non-naturally occurring substances or naturally occurring substances employed by an outside agent to impact a certain alteration of consciousness or bodily systems, etc. etc. From my vantage point I'd advise us to entertain the full scope of the human body, the reach of its mechanisms.

> But we're getting ahead of ourselves. There is a run of show and I am off script.

> Welcome to our drama, our game. I am Marlowe, A Cat. You are the witnesses. Together, dear panel, we must judge tonight's contestants.

> [...]

We can sense Harris's proximity to Jay Wright through a few tacit references that appear on the page even before Marlowe speaks. First, the characters of this "game" all have at least two names, such as BLEVIN AKA TRASH GIRL, WOLF, RAZOR, BOX WINE and SU AKA SMUSH FACE SU, AUTOCORRECT. Even Marlowe's identity is multiple: an AI (programmed by unknown coders) wrapped in a cat's body. Second, there is a metatheatrical level operating around the primary theatrical offering of the drama. We see this in the figure of

Marlowe, whose name calls to mind the Elizabethan playwright famous for his dramatization of Dr. Faustus's dance with Mephistopheles, but also in the opening lines of the AI/Maine coon that acknowledge the presence and participation of the audience. Third, THE HIVE AKA THE FOUNDATION, whom we might identify as a character-set, is described as a "chorus," à la Ancient Greek dramatic χοροί, a feature found in several of Wright's texts. Fourth, as is frequently the case with Wright's plays, the exact placement of the characters and the specifics of the predicament in which they find themselves are unclear. The characters, along with us "witnesses," piece everything together as the play unfolds. With all these similarities, we might understand the subtitle "Approaching Jay Wright" to mean that Harris has chosen to engage with Wright's dramatic texts by tuning into his dramaturgical and syntactical sensibilities.

CODE, however, presents itself differently than Wright's plays, which is to say that it plots a vector that somehow heads toward (i.e., approaches) Wright by departing from his dramaturgy and syntax. Where Wright weaves occult literary references together, for example, Harris splices terms and keywords from the milieu of contemporary social media. Where Wright showcases characters singing ritual incantations, Harris offers an informal rap battle. Where Wright play outside of generic guidelines, Harris utilizes the destabilizing eeriness of Jordan Peele-like comedic horror/suspense. In particular, the suspense mounts as the characters, whom we learn are all on their way to The Foundation to participate in some kind of experiment, wait out a blizzard that has them stranded in a cabin in the middle of nowhere. Things take a turn when Marlowe asks the group, "Is anyone familiar with the parable of the wise assassin?" Together with the abundant references to Wright's plays, these differences, which all showcase Harris's skills as a playwright, provide new points of access into Wright's dramatic texts, ones not clearly visible when the main form of criticism comes through philosophico-literary analysis.

Finally, though his essay appears directly after this introduction, Matthew Goulish turns his dramaturgical eye toward the first play from vol. 1 of *Selected Plays, Passage*. Goulish's remarks were initially prepared for a staged reading of the first ten pages of *Passage* that took place in Chicago in the fall of 2022. On the one hand, then, the "note" he presents here might be understood as helping to contextualize the words and action of the play within several larger themes that, in a way, organize those words and actions. On the other hand, such a neat division between text and context is neither advisable nor possible when approaching Wright's plays. Aware of this, Goulish prefaces his remarks with a comment on research:

> Every reference to an outside source, unattributed in the writing, requires recognition on the part of the reader. Thus research conforms to the limits of the re-searcher. I cannot comment on those references that do not, or have not yet, presented themselves to me as such, because of the constraints on my reading, my knowledge, my time. I make no claims to comprehensivity. One begins with what one knows and proceeds in the faith that the unknown will begin to unfold from it. I offer a practice of dramaturgy—the study of the avenues that begin inside of a theatrical text and lead outside of it—with this philosophy in mind.

This self-reflexive maneuver serves as a helpful guide for all of us who will pick up Wright's plays and attempt to bring them to life upon a stage. We will all feel overwhelmed. We will sense that there is "too much" to bring forth. And yet, hopefully, we can continue to proceed in faith and learn more about texts through the bodies and staging practices that enliven Wright's words for the benefits of an audience.

SPEED AND DELAY: WRIGHT AND CONTEMPORARY THEATER

The appearance of Jay Wright's plays right now, in this moment, is significant for at least three reasons. First, the plays provide a vantage point from which to re-appraise the poetry of this lauded American thinker. The dramatic prose of the playtexts, amplified through the fluidity of the characters' (and actors') speech, offer a counterpoint to the taut poetic verse for which Wright is well known. In a certain sense, this dramatic prose is not new. Wright has been slipping plays into his poetry for many years, such as the dialogue between M_1, M_2, and M_3 in *The Presentable Art of Reading Absence* (2008) and the "dramatic poem" titled "MacIntrye, the Captain and the Saints," which appears in *Explications/Interpretations* (1984). He also provided us with "The Geometry of Rhythm" in *The Prime Anniversary* (2019), a play that explicitly utilizes theatricality to mobilize many of the philosophical concepts we spy in seed form within the preceding poetic verses. With *Selected Plays* vols. 1 and 2, however, the plays stand on their own and beckon directly to theater artists whose capacities as world makers are needed to bring the texts to life. This world-making power has always been nascent within Wright's poetry, but it is primed and ready to be unleashed with new intensity thanks to the plays.

Second, aligned with the work currently undertaken in the field of performance philosophy, the plays present readers and spectators with an opportunity to re-think precisely what thinking is and could be. As Goulish and I endeavored to demonstrate in *Pitch and Revelation*, Wright's poetry constitutes a mode of thought, one that removes or artfully ignores artificial boundaries between fields of knowledge that have been erected by academic disciplines, thereby helping readers access the great weave of the world. With the publishing of *Soul and Substance: A Poet's Examination Papers* (2023), we find another version of this same thinking practice, one that utilizes not poetic verse but poetical prose. As with his poetry and his "examinations," Wright's plays continue to take the pulse of the One, but the presence of the actors' bodies and the aesthetic arrangement of the theatrical setting give us something new. Specifically, they encourage us to see performance *as* thought, theater *as* thinking. This matters now when the place of the arts and humanities within higher education continues to be threatened and when erudition and sophistication gains less and less traction within the world of popular culture. Perhaps Wright's plays can provide remedies to both problems?

Third, these plays are appearing in print during the COVID pandemic. The live art of theater and performance has, in a certain sense, suffered greatly due to restrictions placed on in-person gatherings. At the same time, however, theater has benefited from this challenge posed to its liveness. Online performances, for example, have provided access to theater events that have either been prohibitively expensive to a large number of would-be audience members or staged in parts of the world that made attendance for many unthinkable (or both of these things). Despite the apparent desire to "return to normal," theater-makers would do well to challenge that word "normal" and continue to question what theater could look like if some of its "necessary" components were either removed or tampered with creatively. What would happen if, for example, not just in the case of devised theater, we slowed the theater-making process way down, emphasized the thinking process that takes place during the creation of a given performance, and then incorporated the (dramaturgical, philosophical) thinking of the creation process into the performance and its afterlife? The disruption of theater-as-usual caused by COVID allowed for questions like this to arise, and, certainly when applied to Wright's dramatic texts, questions like this could help reinvigorate the art of staging plays.

Many of the essays in this volume either explicitly emphasize or tacitly express the need to sift carefully through the sedimented history of ideas alive within Wright's plays. Goulish's essay in particular, with its emphasis on dramaturgical preparation, helps us understand the benefits of thinking deeply about Wright's plays:

> I have attempted with these notes as much as possible to avoid interpretation. I mean to say that my descriptive efforts [...] might offer something other than interpretation of the meanings of those actions and moments. That 'other than interpretation' or 'other than meaning,' could take the form of a simple deceleration, a slowing down to regard the cultural, linguistic, and even imagistic depth of resonance at work in the language. The play that proceeds at its pace has no time for this slowing down, which is another way of saying that the slowing down must happen outside of the play, in counter motion to the particulars of its time signature. That's the nature and problem of theater, of performance: it never stops.

Attuning ourselves to the thinking that Wright's plays enact, in other words, brings us to a dual movement. Theater becomes itself through performance. That act of becoming happens so quickly that we, as audience members, might feel as though we're being pulled along against the desires of our minds, which, astride the performance's becoming, seek to make meaning of what we're experiencing. The meaning-making activity tries to drive stakes into the ground and, in vain, hold the performance in place.

An example of this dual movement—becoming/emplacement—shows up in the early pages of Book 2 of Marcel Proust's *À la recherche du temps perdu*, translated into English as *Within a Budding Grove*. There, the narrator plunges into his memory of his first visit to the live theater. Having longed to attend for such a long time and, in the process, having developed an intellectual understanding of what theater is and how it must surely be, the narrator, as a boy, finds himself surprised while watching a staged performance of *Phèdre*. He finds it all to move too quickly.

> I listened to her [Berma, the leading actress] as though I were reading *Phèdre* [...] I could have wished, so as to be able to explore them fully, so as to attempt to discover what it was in them that was beautiful, to arrest, to immobilise for a time before my senses every intonation of the artist's voice, every expression of her features; at least I did attempt, by dint of my mental agility in having, before a line came, my attention ready and tuned to catch it [...] But how short their duration was! Scarcely had a sound been received by my ear than it was displaced there by another.[36]

It would not be difficult to exchange *Phèdre* for any of Wright's selected plays and Proust's narrator for ourselves.

But Goulish actually provides us with another way to participate in the dual movement of live theater performance and meaning making. According to the model he provides, we need not, as Proust's narrator's younger iteration tries to do, strain to unpack each reference as it arises

[36] Marcel Proust, *Within a Budding Grove*, trans. C.K. Scott-Moncrieff (New York: Modern Library, 1924), 26.

so as to appreciate not only the poetic thought motivating the choice of words but also the actor's art that breathes life into the speech housing the reference. Rather, in a sense, we dilate the present moment of performance; we extend the duration of the theatrical event to encompass the times prior to and beyond the staging.

Let us call the prior time "dramaturgy" and the beyond time "the contemporary." Within dramaturgy, we map the sounds and sights offered up throughout the dramatic text and all of its relevant intertexts. In a sense, this introduction I am attempting to conclude instantiates the dramaturgy of this volume of essays. Within the contemporary, we live into the realizations that our minds and bodies have accumulated thanks to the temporalities of dramaturgy and the unfolding performance of the dramatic text. If there is anything like "making sense" of theater, it comes in the contemporary when we discover whether we are worthy of what has befallen us. Dramaturgy, by contrast, does not make sense. Rather, it proposes and describes.

Thinking in this way helps us understand the performance itself as neither dramaturgy nor the contemporary but, rather, delay. Here, "delay" is not identical with its etymology. Instead, it acquires the meaning proposed of it by Marcel Duchamp in his manifesto, "Kind of Sub-Title":

> Use "delay" instead of picture or painting; picture on glass becomes delay in glass—but delay in glass does not mean picture on glass—It's merely a way of succeeding in no longer thinking that the thing in question is a picture—to make a delay of it in the most general way possible, not so much in the different meanings in which delay can be taken, but rather in their indecisive reunion "delay"—a delay in glass as you would say a poem in prose or a spittoon in silver.[37]

This delay is an event of refraction. The event of our perception, which includes the memories we bring to the act of sensing, collides with the

37 Marcel Duchamp, "Kind of Sub-Title," in Mary Ann Caws, ed., *Manifesto: A Century of Isms* (Lincoln: University of Nebraska Press, 2001), 324.

event of that which we perceive. In the collision a change takes place, one that exceeds the imagined control (i.e. intention) of the artist and the intellect of the observer. Duchamp's delay opens a space of encounter that permits virtualities and actualities alike to come to light.

It is my hope that the performances of Wright's plays create such a delay and that we who attend them partake of both dramaturgical and contemporary time in order to help rethink what theater might be. For now, however, in the essays and creative responses that follow, it is perhaps enough to turn primarily toward the dramaturgical, in Goulish's sense, in order to find points of access into the texts compiled in *Selected Plays*, vols. 1 and 2.

SEVEN DRAMATURGICAL NOTES ON *PASSAGE*

Matthew Goulish

A dramaturg's role involves research, and research informs this brief survey of seven notes and background on certain ideas and images that become apparent in Jay Wright's play *Passage*, the first selection in the first of two volumes of selected plays. When I say that certain ideas and images "become apparent," I mean to me. Every reference to an outside source, unattributed in the writing, requires recognition on the part of the reader. Thus research conforms to the limits of the researcher. I cannot comment on those references that do not, or have not yet, presented themselves to me as such, because of the constraints on my reading, my knowledge, my time. I make no claims to comprehensivity. One begins with what one knows and proceeds in the faith that the unknown will begin to unfold from it. I offer a practice of dramaturgy — the study of the avenues that begin inside of a theatrical text and lead outside of it — with this philosophy in mind.

IN THE MONOLOGUE which begins the play, Bursach speaks of reading the metaphysics of John the Scot, and of how this aligns with something he has been saying to Francisco Hernández. He says this while preparing to smoke a cigar. I will address Francisco Hernández and then John the Scot, but first the cigar.

1. SOLITUDE OF THE CUBE

To quote Will Daddario, "*Passage* is one of if not *the* most autobiographical of the plays in these volumes. For example, I was talking to Jay a few weeks ago and he said he had been sitting out back, in the garden, in Vermont, smoking a cigar. Lois has mentioned that he smokes cigars only when he is reading about prime numbers or other mathematical issues." Will has set the scene for us, since this play begins this way. After a brief somewhat confused exchange between Bursach and Chalana, Bursach clarifies that he is talking about "the one who proposed the solitude of the cube."[1]

This refers to the book *Soledad al Cubo* (2001) by contemporary Mexican poet Francisco Hernández, the poet with whom Bursach, in his opening monologue, says he had been speaking, a friend to whom he refers using the familiar name Paco. *Soledad al Cubo* has to my knowledge not been translated from the Spanish, so I will leave this first note here. We immediately encounter the broad, international erudition of this American writer, Jay Wright. Bursach, the central character (although that centrality at times experiences degrees of slippage) reflects Wright's international scope and apparently, in fictional form, interacts bilingually with a real-life poet. We note how, in order to appreciate the depth of this play, we need to look, even if only for a moment, outside of its frame.

2. JOHN DUNS SCOTUS

Bursach has made a connection between Hernández's solitude of the cube and the metaphysics of John the Scot, and he and Chalana banter about this philosopher's work, with which she also apparently has great familiarity. Bursach soon quotes the philosopher precisely when he answers one of her questions with a statement.

> CHALANA: Whose poetry? What would John the Scot say?
>
> BURSACH: I thought you knew. You accused me of judgment, some assertion of truth. What would he say? "All the attributes of being are virtually included in being and in those things that come under being." How is that? I'm not losing everything. No, sir, I can remember some things, things that make sense.[2]

The quoted sentence, with the phrase "are virtually included in," introduces the concept of the virtual into the landscape of the play.

1 Wright, *Selected Plays*, vol. 1, 8.
2 *Selected Plays*, vol. 1, 9.

John Faber Sr., *John Duns Scotus*, early 18th century. Mezzotint, 13⅞" × 9⅞"
London, National Portrait Gallery.

John Duns Scotus is the Latinized version of the name John Duns
the Scot. Duns Scotus is commonly used to refer to the medieval
Franciscan philosopher and theologian who lived from 1266 to 1308.
I associate him primarily with haecceity, or the principal of "thisness,"
individuation or distinctness, a concept of uniqueness under which

only one object falls—separating one horse from other horses, one leaf from other leaves, one human from other humans. Scotus's ethics reflected this emphasis on the significance of individual uniqueness in relation to how knowledge works, as well as its implications for metaphysics (the study of first and abstract principles such as being, time, and causation). Scotus's ethics was understood in its time as resisting a fatalistic view of an omnipotent God.

His thought is one of the principal foundations for Gilles Deleuze's philosophy, especially in Deleuze's 1968 work *Difference and Repetition*. Because of Duns Scotus, Deleuze holds identity not as a first but as a second principle, as a principle of *becoming*, or the individual becoming an identity. Identity is always a more general concept than individual; all individuals differ, but all identities repeat. Deleuze considered haecceity as applying not only to individuals or objects, but also to events: each wind, each day, each hour, distinguishes itself as individual and does not repeat. Deleuze credited Duns Scotus with replacing "the model of judgment with that of the proposition."[3]

These concepts are key for understanding Jay Wright's poetry, manifestations of character in his plays, and certain turns in the dialogue of *Passage*, as well as the unfolding of identities in the play.

I will close this note with the reminder that conservative scholastic medieval philosophers held Scotus in low regard. Thus the term Duns became synonymous with a simpleton who followed Scotus's teachings. It gives us the word dunce and perhaps even the "dunce cap," modeled on John the Scot's headwear.

3. DEEP SONG BY ANTONIO MACHADO

Near the start of his intervention into, and disruption of, Bursach's vigil of watching the neighbor's house as requested by Chalana, Pierre recites two unexplained lines in Spanish. This recitation serves as his way of identifying himself to Bursach.

3 Gilles Deleuze, *Difference and Repetition* (New York: Columbia University Press, 1994), 35.

"Y era la muerte, al hombro la cuchilla,
el paso largo, torva y esquelética."[4]

These lines derive from a poem titled *Cante Hondo* by the poet Antonio Machado. The Spanish Civil War and Franco's rise to power exiled Machado to Southern France in the very last months of his life. I will reproduce this short poem translated into English by Paul Burns and Salvador Ortiz-Carboneres, with the title *Deep Song.* I will italicize the lines that Pierre speaks.

Wrapped in myself and thought, I was
unpicking threads of weariness and gloom,
when through the windows of my room,
open to a summer night,
my ears caught the lament
of a dreamy ballad, fractured
by the brooding tremolos
of the magic music of my land.
      And it was Love, like a red flame…
A taut hand on the vibrant string
formed a long golden sigh,
which became a spurt of stars.
      And it was Death, scythe on shoulder
long-leggèd, skeletal, grim
just as in my childhood dreams.
      And on the guitar, resonant, quivering,
the brusque hand, drumming, made the sound
of a coffin hitting the ground.
      And the lonely lament was a gust
that fans the ashes and scatters the dust.

The recited couplet positions Pierre in some near proximity to death, as either himself a personification of the reaper imagined in childhood fears, or at least one conversant with these precise lines depicting the

---

4 Wright, *Selected Plays*, vol. 1, 16.

reaper's image, in a relation that perhaps inverts the one referred to with Paco that converses with Bursach in the vernaculars of poetry.

4. " ... THE OLD FRED HARVEY'S AT THE TRAIN STATION."

Roughly halfway through the play, after the fourth character, Agnes, who will become Margaret (just as Pierre will become Francis and then Malachi), has made her entrance, a whimsical *coup de théâtre* divides the action.

> PIERRE *and* CHALANA *ride on in a toy engine car and caboose.*

This miniature train dominates the second half of the play as it shuttles the characters offstage in pairs. This device facilitates permutations of duets within the quartet of characters, recombining the dialogue into nearly every possible variation like a Bach fugue. One question concerns us here, however: why a train?

The theatrical idiom of this play treats instances of the language of memory, in particular memories that seem to carry with them some unfinished business, as propositions. These propositions then generate actualizations or material manifestations of the images, somewhat transformed, that made their debut in such speech acts of recollection. Certain words return, echoing in the world as a figure, an object, or a machine. Francis refers to the little train as "my machine." It presents us with a diminished version of the railway culture that made its appearance in Bursach's garden soliloquy ten pages earlier.

> You know, this reminds me of sitting on our porch in Albuquerque, New Mexico, watching the sun set and the pigeons coming to roost on the old Fred Harvey's at the train station.[5]

The Fred Harvey Company provided hospitality along the route of the Atchison, Topeka and Santa Fe Railway, which included a major junction in Albuquerque. The Harvey Company began this venture in

5 Wright, *Selected Plays*, vol. 1, 2. The Fred Harvey imagery returns and becomes important in Wright's *Delights of Memory* cycle of plays. See Michael Paul Berlin's essay in this collection for a brief elaboration.

Fred Harvey Meals
Santa Fe

1876. It catered to train passengers with restaurant and hotel services, recognizable in presentation throughout the various regions of the country. Each of their elaborately designed buildings situated alongside train stations became a landmark oasis for travelers. After the death of Fred, the entrepreneurial founder, the Harvey family continued the business until its sale in 1968.

One last detail bears mentioning, in reference to Bursach's self-description at the end of this same speech, noted above, a richly detailed memory of the garden.

> Certainly, there were the willows, and juniper, and quaking aspen. They were the breeze; they were the shade. And there were lilacs and roses and rhododendron, and I'll swear there was birchleaf buckthorn and blue violet, and a strange little thing called a balloon flower. That might not be the garden I saw, but one I wanted. Did I say wanted? Hey, you don't think a little colored boy from the other side of the tracks could have anything to say about gardens in the great Fred Harvey's yard, do you? No, that's fantasy, I've just told you a lie.[6]

The company maintained the famous uniformed Harvey Girls, who oversaw the public-facing services, as a racially segregated staff, enforcing a "white only" policy of hiring.

5. BORGES AND MIRRORS

Soon after the toy train has removed Bursach and Agatha from the stage and left Chalana and Francis (formerly Pierre) together, as Francis begins his mutation into Malachi ("My mother called me Malachi.") Chalana asks him, "Do you believe in Borges?" He answers her with his own question, "Who, or what, is this Borges?" Francis apparently lacks Pierre's literary acumen. Chalana's monologue defining Jorge Luis Borges, the twentieth-century Argentine writer who pioneered a singular mode of essay-story, includes a reference to the writer's blindness which developed late in life. She then says, "I wonder what

---

6 Wright, *Selected Plays*, vol. 1, 11.

the man who spent so much of his life engaged with mirrors would say."[7] In this section we will consider Chalana's statement of wonder.

Borges's emblematic works continually circulated around a narrow range of themes or images. It further defines the cosmology of *Passage* when Chalana introduces into the dialogue not only Borges, but also the Borgesian mirror, his obsessive fear of reflection and duplication. Her maneuver makes a glancing reference to Pierre, if not Francis, as a time-delayed reflection of Bursach, as well as to the triplet of figures Pierre, Francis, and Malachi, and their mutual image as an instance of Borgesian "spectral duplication." The play's superpositional texture of overlapping themes has begun to make its density apparent.

We can isolate the Borgesian mirror with this distillation from the first paragraph of the three-paragraph microfiction *The Draped Mirrors* from his 1964 book *Dreamtigers*,[8] translated by Mildred Boyer and Harold Morland from the Spanish volume *El Hacedor*:

> Islam asserts that on the unappealable day of judgment every perpetrator of the image of a living creature will be raised from the dead with his works, and he will be commanded to bring them to life, and he will fail, and be cast out with them into the fires of punishment. As a child, I felt before large mirrors that same horror of a spectral duplication or multiplication of reality. Their infallible and continuous functioning, their pursuit of my actions, their cosmic pantomime, were uncanny then, whenever it began to grow dark. One of my persistent prayers to God and my guardian angel was that I not dream about mirrors. I know I watched them with misgivings. Sometimes I feared they might begin to deviate from reality; other times I was afraid of seeing there my own face, disfigured by strange calamities.

6. CHALANA'S INCIDENTAL WARPED QUOTATIONS

In the bantering and somewhat conflictual dialogue with Francis that unfolds after the Borges mirror inquiry, Chalana displays a loose phrasing

---

7 All quotes in this paragraph from Wright, *Selected Plays*, vol. 1, 24–25.

8 Jorge Luis Borges, *Dreamtigers* (Austin: U. of Texas Press, 1964), 27.

of three quick, embedded, unacknowledged quotations, each of which she alters slightly and warps to her own purposes. Her more playful counterpoint to the literary turns introduced earlier by Bursach and Pierre demonstrates the same degree of conversancy with a range of texts, yet offers its own acerbic edge and seems to play a part in unbalancing Francis. I will take a moment to trace these three remarks.

> [*Sings.*] "I've grown accustomed to your face." Bursach will never recognize you. Pierre. Francis. Different light.[9]

> What does this mistake mean? There is nothing there that is the case. Do you see what I'm getting at?[10]

> Oh, no. I know what you're thinking. Give it up. What's she to Hecuba? No, Francis, there is a resolution devoutly to be wished, and I refuse to be deprived of my contemplation.[11]

The triad of references offers an indirect portrait of Chalana by way of the language artifacts that she has absorbed into her speech from *My Fair Lady*, *Tractatus Logico-Philosophicus*, and *Hamlet*.

She first makes use of the musical *My Fair Lady* (1956) and Henry Higgins's mournful ballad of missing Eliza Doolittle who has fled his callous tutorship.

> I've grown accustomed to her face
> She almost makes the day begin
> I've grown accustomed to the tune that
> She whistles night and noon
> Her smiles, her frowns
> Her ups, her downs
> Are second nature to me now
> Like breathing out and breathing in
> I was serenely independent and content before we met
> Surely I could always be that way again—

9 Wright, *Selected Plays*, vol. 1, 24.
10 *Selected Plays*, vol. 1, 25.
11 *Selected Plays*, vol. 1, 26.

> And yet
> I've grown accustomed to her look
> Accustomed to her voice
> Accustomed to her face

Chalana changes the "her" to "your" in the lyric, and casts herself as the professor of phonetics invented by George Bernard Shaw in the play *Pygmalion* (1913), source for the Lerner and Loewe musical.

Next she inverts the first line of Wittgenstein's 1922 landmark work *Tractatus Logico-Philosophicus.*

I   The world is everything that is the case.

I.I   The world is the totality of facts, not of things.

I.II   The world is determined by the facts, and by these being *all* the facts.

Chalana offers a negation of the Austrian philosopher's initial proposition as a challenge to Francis: "There is nothing there that is the case."

Finally she rounds off the dialogic volley with a double dose from Shakespeare, both lines spoken by the Danish Prince. First in his rueful speech that closes Act II bemoaning the plays of tragedy after speaking to the troupe of stage actors, in reference to the tragedy *Hecuba* by Euripides, Hamlet soliloquizes:

> Tears in his eyes, distraction in's aspect
> A broken voice, and his whole function suiting
> With forms to his conceit? and all for nothing!
> For Hecuba?
> What's Hecuba to him or he to Hecuba,
> That he should weep for her?

Chalana reverses the gender of the question, "What's she to Hecuba," then follows with a fragment from the next soliloquy that begins Act III.

> To be, or not to be,—that is the question:—
> Whether 'tis nobler in the mind to suffer
> The slings and arrows of outrageous fortune,
> Or to take arms against a sea of troubles,

> And by opposing end them?—To die,—to sleep,—
> No more, and by a sleep to say we end
> The heart-ache and the thousand natural shocks
> That flesh is heir to,—'tis a consummation
> Devoutly to be wish'd.

Rather than a consummation, Chalana offers a resolution devoutly to be wished, refusing to be deprived of her contemplation. Francis responds in apparent desperation, as Chalana completes his transformation into his next iteration of character, Malachi.

> FRANCIS: My god, I think Chalana thinks she can design her own entrapment. Where the hell is Bursach?
>
> CHALANA: Do I frighten you, Malachi?[12]

7. THE BOOK OF JOB

I will conclude the brief and cursory notes that I have sketched here with a consideration of a turn in the dialogue near the play's end in which Francis and Bursach engage in a biblical call and response.

> CHALANA: Bursach, I sense an accusation. They think we've conjured a place that doesn't exist.
>
> BURSACH: No, Chalana. They're mistaken. *This* place doesn't exist. You see how clever they are? They've caught us out. Chalana. Bursach. A couple of innocents too dumb to understand the claims upon them.
>
> FRANCIS: And here, church, he starts the false confession that relieves him of responsibility.
>
> BURSACH: "Tell me, if you have understanding."
>
> FRANCIS: Who "laid the foundation of the earth?" Not you, Bursach. Don't pretend. With all your talk of joy.
>
> BURSACH: Will you take that away from me, too?[13]

12 Wright, *Selected Plays*, vol. 1, 26.
13 *Selected Plays*, vol. 1, 35–36.

In the exchange, cued almost impossibly by the slightest suggestion, one completes the other's thought, supplying the preceding line in the referenced passage.

This moment in the dialogue alludes to the profound originary theodicy, when Job has called out to God for justification for all that he has suffered and for the boundlessness of human misery. God's speech commences in Chapter 38.

> Then the Lord answered Job out of the whirlwind:
> "Who is this that darkens counsel by words without knowledge?
> Gird up your loins like a man,
> I will question you, and you shall declare to me.
> Where were you when I laid the foundation of the earth?
> Tell me, if you have understanding.
> Who determined its measurements—surely you know!
> Or who stretched the line upon it?
> On what were its bases sunk, or who laid its cornerstone,
> when the morning stars sang together,
> and all the sons of God shouted for joy?"

God's reprimand to Job invokes and extends the metaphor of the earth as architecture, with a foundation and a cornerstone, or as a surveyed structure, as the question "Or who stretched the line upon it?" attests. In his early poems regarding Benjamin Banneker, Jay Wright has plumbed the metaphorical possibilities of surveying and city construction, no doubt informed by this deific monologue. Here Francis returns Bursach's challenge with an adversarial riposte undermining Bursach's "talk of joy," as both turn the verse to their own intentions. The uniformity of their shared reservoir of language reminds us of Chalana's invocation of the mirror, in its Borgesian instance, of multiplying a single entity into a form turned against itself, a menacing reversal of Scotus's haecceity.

✳ ✳ ✳

I have attempted with these notes as much as possible to avoid interpretation. I mean to say that my descriptive efforts—to include wider views of those precise landscapes indicated by lines of dialogue that

I recognize as reaching outside of the confines of the play's action and moment—might offer something other than interpretation of the meanings of those actions and moments. That "other than interpretation" or "other than meaning," could take the form of a simple deceleration, a slowing down to regard the cultural, linguistic, and even imagistic depth of resonance at work in the language. The play that proceeds at its pace has no time for this slowing down, which is another way of saying that the slowing down must happen outside of the play, in counter motion to the particulars of its time signature. That's the nature and problem of theater, of performance: it never stops. Thus these notes operate as a pre-show announcement, an extended rumination on preconditionality. We cannot arrest the instant of a thought as it makes itself visible on the stage and then passes away. We can only prepare ourselves to receive it. The stage is not a page after all, nor does it aspire to be. The degree to which this writer understands that proposition defines one key difference between his poetry and his plays. I will leave on that note and the elementary instance of polysemy, or the coexistence of many possible and correct meanings (signs) within a single word—a key concept for all of Wright's writing—that we find when we recognize the play at work in the play.

WHAT I SEE IN *HOMAGE TO ANTHONY BRAXTON*

Devin King

In spite of the fact the earth is reputed
to be a ball, the formality stops there.

—Edward Dorn, "What I See in *The Maximus Poems*"

THE ONLY TIME I have seen Jay Wright read was at the greatest little bookstore in the upper middle west: Milwaukee's Woodland Pattern. Wright doesn't like his readings recorded, so I'll only tell you two things about the evening: (1) Jay's wife, Lois, noticed I was wearing a quartz watch and asked me what time it was and (2) pretty quickly into what was a pretty normal poetry reading, Wright began acting out a play. Voices mostly, not really moving around, though you could see the energy of a performer crackling in slight motions that did not seem to be authentic to Wright but to those of his characters. It was not a perfect performance but it was honest, as if five minutes before the reading Wright said to himself, I'd like to act out a play today. Only Wright, and maybe Lois, knows how much foreknowledge Wright had of what he was going to read.

The gesture is reversed in the two-volume collection of Wright's plays that this essay, part of a third volume of responses, is attached. *Homage to Anthony Braxton* sounds like the title of a poem rather than the title of a play. It's a nice sleight of hand and changes the stakes of the play from, "let's watch (or read) a play" to "what does the American experimental composer Anthony Braxton have to do with any of this?"

There isn't an answer that comes directly from the play—consistent with opacity, an aspect of Wright's poetics—though there might be a few answers if you were to, say, meditate on the play, Wright's own poetics, and what you might know about Anthony Braxton. Like his poetry, Wright's plays are plain-spoken and gesturally transparent, even if their inner meaning can often be unclear to the critic, if not the audience member. Writing about Wright's work—saying something about Wright's work—is easiest for the enthusiast speaking breathlessly after watching a performance or reading a book of poems. The critic who speaks from the position of binding and naming might be reminded of what Basil Bunting, with a "pixy-like smile," said to the critic Carroll Terrell after eating "a huge tureen filled with a stew with Polish sausage and winter vegetables" and "a heavy garlic sauce which had a consistency heavier than sour cream" (all cooked by Thomas Meyer and washed down with a Balkan cabernet and Bruichladdich Islay Scotch): "You're not a poet, you're a predator." Wright offers a take on interpreting his poetry in an interview with Charles Rowell:

> The poems do ask you to enter a process that requires thought, intuition, memory, factual and imaginative comprehension. I wouldn't use the word surrender; it's better to say that you are asked to accept the poem's challenge and to listen to, walk along, sing along and be with the poem. You are right in saying that you're asked "to become" with the voices. You are also asked to understand, and one thing you will understand in the process of entering in…you will understand one process of entering, and that understanding should make you aware of the many ways and complexities of entering.[1]

To enter the play, I'd like to walk along the play. Here's my synopsis of *Homage to Anthony Braxton*. Yours may differ.

Hank Huitt—Black, 45 yrs old—and Annie Lewis—Black, 35 yrs old—walk into Liberation Park, somewhere in a large city in present day America. Annie is a prostitute, Hank is a hustler, and they're drinking, carrying on. Johnny Walker—Black, mid-twenties—comes into the park, selling plastic lions to fundraise for Pastor Ames, who is running for city council. Hank borrows a couple of bucks from Annie

1 Charles H. Rowell, "'The Unraveling of the Egg': An Interview with Jay Wright," in "Jay Wright: A Special Issue," *Callaloo* 19 (Autumn 1983): 7.

and sarcastically gives the money to Walker as if he was a beggar, and makes an angry show of refusing the lions in return, much to Walker's dismay, who gives the lions to Annie instead. Walker lets Hank and Annie know that the Pastor will be having a rally the next day, and leaves.

Dobie Thomas—Black, 40 yrs old—enters pushing a shopping cart loaded with signs and other ephemera for the Pastor's rally. Hank tries to borrow money from Dobie to pay Annie back and is refused. Hank gets angry, grabs the lions from Annie and stomps on them. Hank rifles through Dobie's cart, and begins reading the Pastor's literature, with great sarcasm and anger:

> [*…reading…*] "He delivered me, because he delighted in me." [*He slowly redoes the roll, slowly and thoughtfully puts it back.*] Is that true, Dobie? [*Turning quickly on him.*] What? Who is this he? Who is goin' to pull me out of this evil shit I have to suffer day by day? *He* understands it? *He* delights in me? And the Reverend Benjamin Ames knows this? How did he get the key, Dobie? That's what I can't stand about that nigger, Annie. He's a scholar of the soul, souls he ain't never seen, souls he wouldn't recognize if they came to him in gingham and sunshine. [*He starts to rummage in the cart again.*] Ain't there somethin' in here about love? Got to be somethin' about love.[2]

The quote is one of a few centering moments of what is, otherwise, a series of insistent blow-ups and nastiness emanating from Hank. We've seen two or three of these moments so far, more to come. This speech focuses a careful consideration on where Hank's anger might *really* come from, a frustration with what Holden Caulfield calls phonies, albeit from a place of wizened adulthood rather than the angry gropings of a teenager. But, then, it's also reflexive critique by Wright of a critic who might ask the same question as Hank: "Ain't there somethin' in [this] here [play] about love?"

Dobie puts the Pastor's sundries behind the band-stage and parks the cart, with two crates, under the stage. Hank gets angry at Dobie—for "undertak[ing] to do somethin' for people who spit on [him]"—and then

2 Wright, *Selected Plays*, vol. 2, 96.

at Annie, who tries to leave to go to work. Hank then asks the two of them if they want to make some money, and they gather in as Tommy Johnson—Black, mid-twenties—enters, selling clothes. Hank lightly tries to convince him to dump the clothes into Dobie's cart, and then climbs on the stage, sits in the chair on the stage and begins a speech that ends with:

> Now, move your eyes slowly all around you. What do you see? I'll tell you what you see. You see nothin' but black. You're black. Call on God, or cuss his name. You're black. If you walked here, or came in a Cadillac, you're black. If you hustle for the man, or hustle back in the alley, you're black. If you eat hogmaws, grits and cornbread, or eat steak, salad and Dutch toast, you're black. If you grin all the time, or look like you'd chomp into a bear, you're black. If you're bright as marble, yellow as a sunflower, brown as sugar, black as a starless night, you're black. You're black. Let's get that straight now.[3]

Anthony Braxton, like many of his colleagues in the Association for the Advancement of Creative Musicians, has historically been frustrated by the inability of critics and audiences to position his music outside of jazz, ignoring the broad range of Braxton's influences, and the various art, philosophical, and other world histories Braxton engages with as an artist. Wright might be said to feel—or to have felt, the laziness around notions like these has changed quite a bit in the past twenty years—similar pressure from within the poetry community. Above my desk, below the window that I look out into my backyard in Santa Fe, filled sometimes with a family of bobcats but more often with a northern flicker that likes the suet I put out, is a quote I copied out of a book written by Braxton, typing it in Chicago on an index card with a typewriter I'd bought in Boston: "...all the musics that are close to the community and allow for individual presence bring out this dichotomy between the rational system and the three dimensional system."

What I think Braxton is saying here, or have begun to think as I've looked at this index card daily for what must be at least half-a-dozen years

3 Wright, *Selected Plays*, vol. 2, 102.

now—and I'm sorry but I can't cite the quote for you or give you its larger context (though it must have come from somewhere early on in the *Tri-Axium Writings*)—is that creating a performance space that allows the individual performer to come into consistent, though not necessarily violent, conflict with a larger community of individuals allows us to thread the needle between the categories we use for thinking—the rational system—and those objects that the world presents to us—the three dimensional system. After a bit of back and forth with Annie,

> HANK: …What can he, the Reverend Benjamin Ames, tell you that the unholy Henry the Hank Huitt can't? That you have been given the burden of wearin' the thorny crown of your skin? That you will never be free? That you can only be free? I been studyin' it. [*He holds up his hand.*] Prophecy. The end of the world will not come. No one will lose. But the only winners will be those who know how to move on without runnin' away. You see what I'm sayin'. There is no way out.[4]

Here's how Anthony Braxton's essay "Narrative Structures" ends:

> More and more it is becoming possible to see the difference between art experiences based on fundamental constructs of recognition as opposed to the newer contemporary "elastic" models that are couched in brilliant philosophical terms but somehow can't address itself to the "linear-sustained" interest/attraction (associations) that narrative architecture has long demonstrated. This to me is one of the important challenges of the closing twentieth century—that is, the need to re-establish re-structural composite narrative structures that can serve the need of our citizens in the next time cycle. Rather than simply seek to throw everything from the past away—as if nothing from our recorded experiences has any transferral [*sic.*] relevance—the challenge of the next time cycle will call for fresh attempts to "merge" a composite myth-narrative base that can be both flexible and stable according to the needs of the "experiencer"…[5]

4 *Selected Plays*, vol. 2, 103.

5 Braxton, "Narrative Structures," *Anthony Braxton Research Papers*, https://tricentricfoundation.org/anthony-braxton-narrative-structures.

Like Wright's plays—most of which, even the "experimental" ones, are closer in form to normative modes of contemporary American theater than, say, the variant techniques of post-Cageian performance—Braxton refuses the total refusal of what he calls the myth-narrative structure—i.e., something like story. Braxton continues: "the concept of 'poetic-logics' architecture is an attempt to fuse the structural logo of a given focus with a dramatic 'under-sense' that can allow for ritual identification (and alignment)." I take this dramatic under-sense to mean a lack of a final dramatic context that focuses the audience-member into what might be called catharsis. Wright and Braxton create a narrative—a dramatic—playing field where the audience member is asked, with some slight level of improvisational freedom given focus by the structure of Braxton's scores or Wright's narratives, in Wright's words, "to accept the poem's challenge and to listen to, walk along, sing along and be with the poem, to play in, to walk along."

Hank offers Tommy the chair to speak. Tommy refuses, and then Hank convinces him to show up tomorrow night, at the rally, where they will sell Tommy's clothes out of the cart. Annie and Hank exit together, Dobie and Tommy exit.

Walker enters and goes to the back of the bandstand. Dobie, Tommy, and Annie enter with the loaded cart. Tommy sees Walker and tries to sell him some clothes. Walker refuses. Through various machinations Tommy is able to wrap Walker up in a coat while Dobie and Annie take the purse containing the Pastor's fundraising money. Walker exits. There's some grumbling about how to split the take, Tommy believes that he thought up the hustle and has earned a larger share. Dobie and Annie disagree, Annie is especially angry because she "sold [him] half [her] night already." They split it even. Tommy exits and Dobie asks Annie if they can keep the money secret from Hank:

ANNIE: …When you gonna stop foolin' yourself, Dobie?[6]

They exit. The stage darkens. Two unnamed men shoot dice. Walker enters and asks if they've seen Tommy, Dobie, and Annie. They say no and

6 Wright, *Selected Plays*, vol. 2, 113.

then accuse him of being a narc. Walker tries to appear hip by singing a blues. This makes the two men angrier, and the first man grabs Walker.

SECOND MAN: You ain't one 'a them gone off on Jesus, is you?

FIRST MAN: Naw, this ain't no minister, man. A minister talk about my soul. He stomp around and say I eat too much of the hog. That my whiskey brand is gon blind me...[7]

Things get more uncomfortable. The men question whether Walker is really Black, and try to get him to taste their ribs and liquor. Walker refuses until they force him to eat and drink.

FIRST MAN: ... Aw, I'm sorry we ain't got no Johnny Walker Red, brother.

[WALKER *stops at the mention of his name.*]

What's the matter?

JOHNNY: Nothin'. I just remembered someone.

FIRST MAN: Who?

JOHNNY: Me.[8]

Wright is an artist that downplays his biography as an entry-point to his own work, but I take the fact of his Southwestern upbringing to bear on a few of the plays in these two volumes; there are places named in these plays that are real places, and Wright grew up near them. In *Aria*, another play included in the two-volume collection, the character Sánú has lost their father's ankh:

SÁNÚ: And now you can't find it. This ankh that belongs to my father. Forgive me, Garbh, I know I shouldn't mention this at this time, since you've lost the connection...the relation you claim to have had with my father.

GARBH: I had no connection.[9]

7 *Selected Plays*, vol. 2, 116.
8 *Selected Plays*, vol. 2, 118.
9 *Selected Plays*, vol. 1, 342.

In 2015 or 16, my wife and I began thinking about moving from Chicago to the Southwest. On one of our visits, stuffed with chiles rellenos from The Tune-Up Cafe, we got a realtor to take us to see a few houses outside Santa Fe: one in Lamy, one in Galisteo, one in Eldorado, one in Madrid, and a few in between. My wife and I, frustratingly particular in our openness to just about any type of space as long as it was made with purpose, had laid down a few contrasting ideals based around the artist's life we'd led through our twenties and thirties in the hopes of carrying some part of it into our forties: (1) maybe someplace out of the way but big enough to host artists-in-residence, (2) maybe someplace slightly busy but big enough so we could have a gallery, and (3) oh yeah, we're planning on kids, so maybe someplace with good schools.

Lamy (*lay-me*) has a train station that connects the town to Marfa; there was a weirdly laid out house up on a hill (the town was really only a hill with a train station at the bottom) with a yoga studio that I guess we could have turned into a residency. If non-locals know Galisteo, it is because Agnes Martin lived in the town during the height of her powers; other, more contemporary artists and critics live there but perhaps, like me, you're of a Falstaffian-mien and are more excited that Burl Ives was a resident. I was ready to give the town of 250 an earnest chance—marked by a line of mailboxes, an empty and ancient general store, and church—but was put out by the crumbling house, backed up against another crumbling house, along a creek that every building seemed to be sinking into.

Eldorado is the Southwest's version of a midwestern suburb: twenty minutes southwest of Santa Fe on 25 are 6,000 people, all living in made-to-order single-family houses with a good high school smack dab in the middle of it all. The four-bedroom house our realtor showed us reminded me of Dan's family house, a kid I was in a band with in high school, and then, three doors down the hall, was a room filled to the brim with guitars, amplifiers, drums, all you would need to re-live my life as a teenage huffer of hardcore.

In Madrid (*mad-rid* not *muh-**drid***) our realtor took us to a blue house on the road through town. Wild with coal, when the railroad came through the southwest in the late 1800s, Madrid was built up and owned by the Cerrillos Coal & Iron Co. as a company town for its workers. Famously, most of the housing was dissembled elsewhere, flat-packed, shipped along the Cerrillos Coal Railroad (owned by you know who), and re-assembled in town.

> SÁNÚ: The obscure suggestion of a living light has lost his memory. [*To* LUTTUOSO.] I remind you of that road to Madrid, *monsieur*. You will recall, surely, how you crawled on that desert floor, begging for water.
>
> LUTTUOSO: Hey, don't get nasty with me.
>
> SÁNÚ: Nasty!? I picked you up. I came along in an old Ford, on my way to Santa Fe. How could I miss a dead body in the road? …
>
> LUTTUOSO: … You picked me up … And what did you do?
>
> SÁNÚ: I carried you until I saw your eyes stand still in your head, and then I buried you.
>
> LUTTUOSO: In Santa Fe?
>
> SÁNÚ: No, of course not. That village wouldn't have you. We had to make do with a ditch along the road.[10]

Oscar Huber was the superintendent of the mines—de facto mayor-cum-boss of the town—during Madrid's boom years between 1919 and 1954. The ballpark that's still in town, the first to have lights west of the Mississippi, is named after Oscar. The historian Richard Melzer, in his short *Madrid Revisited*, describes Huber as "a short, bespectacled man." I would also add that he was an evil man.

Believing, as most bosses do, that when workers aren't working, trouble will come, Huber set up the Madrid Employees Club during the darkest days of the Depression to force the town's workers to put on social activities, have them do menial tasks after work, as well as pay dues to the Employee Club out of their already comically low wages (so low that borrowing company scrip at high interest levels to buy goods in town imported by the company and marked up was the only way most workers could afford to live in the town).

10 Wright, *Selected Plays*, vol. 1, 345.

Most famous of the activities put on by the Employees Club was the Madrid Lights, a Christmas celebration covering the town in flickering lights at a time when electricity, especially in that part of the country, was still a lark. Melzer argues that rather than a technique of pacification, the social activities—and the lights especially—were used as an advertisement for the community of Madrid. No one, even life-long miners, wanted to work in Madrid's mines, where "the veins of high grade coal dipped an awkward sixteen degrees into the earth and averaged only 3.5 feet in height…miners in Madrid had to labor with hand tools in small, wet and uncomfortable 'rat holes,' while those in [near-by] Gallup and Raton found veins that were usually over six feet tall and far more accessible."[11] The lights, written about in newspapers in New York, suggested a promising, stable community for those left for dead during the Depression.

[*The men look at him strangely.*]

FIRST MAN: Right. You drinkin'?

11 Richard Melzer, *Madrid Revisited: Life and Labor in a New Mexican Mining Camp in the Years of the Great Depression* (Santa Fe, NM: Lightning Tree, 1976), 14.

[WALKER *does.*]

SECOND MAN: That's more like it. Maybe he do belong to us.

FIRST MAN: Can't tell. [*To* WALKER.] Give me a hit.

[WALKER *gives him the bottle.*]

JOHNNY: Later.

FIRST MAN: Why? We got a whole bottle here.

JOHNNY: You wouldn't understand, my man.

FIRST MAN: [*Comes closer to* WALKER.] Well, school me.

[WALKER *backs away.*]

JOHNNY: Time, brother.

FIRST MAN: I knew you were jive. Well, now we gon teach.

[WALKER *rapidly unbuttons his jacket and starts to go to his belt.* HANK
  has appeared unnoticed from stage right.]

HANK: Hold it! No need to go to the well, my man.[12]

Hank separates the three of them, calms the two unnamed men down, and then sits on a bench with Walker and tries to get him to get rid of his gun. Walker demurs, and Hanks asks him if he's seen Dobie, Annie, or Tommy, and whether the gun is for them. Hank knows they stole money from Walker and is angry that they didn't cut him in on the deal. Walker again demurs, and Hank laughs, telling Walker he got him out of one scrape and he should let Hank help him find Dobie, Annie, and Tommy. The two men argue about how to handle the three of them—Hank seems to have a plan—but Walker angrily gets up to leave. Hank tries to convince him that Walker can "get back that respect" if Walker sets it up with Pastor Ames to allow Hank, Dobie, Annie, and Tommy be the only people selling items in the park during the rally. Walker refuses, and Hank asks who else will help him.

12 Wright, *Selected Plays*, vol. 2, 118.

JOHNNY: ...I know you. Benjamin Ames knows you. Every member of the nation in which I stand knows you. Tell me, now. Don't you have a suspicion of somethin' that's been in this park since we hung that sign? It ought to take your breath away.

HANK: [*Quickly.*] What do you know about that?

JOHNNY: I know love when I see it.

[HANK *realizes his mistake.* WALKER *laughs nervously.*]

Funny. [*He pats his belt.*] I've got this thing because I don't want to be shut out of that love. [*He turns to* HANK.] I'm learnin' to protect that....

HANK: ...I need to know you're on my side.

JOHNNY: The only way you can be on my side is to be with me.[13]

In 1954, an advertisement appeared in the *Wall Street Journal*:

Entire town.
200 houses, grade and high school, power
house, general store, tavern, machine shop,
mineral rights, 9000 acres, excellent climate,
fine industrial location.

13 Wright, *Selected Plays*, vol. 2, 122.

In 1975, unable to sell the entire town, Joe Huber—Oscar's son—put the 150 buildings that made up Madrid as individual units for sale. The entire town sold in sixteen days.

JOHNNY: I love your analysis, brother. I have to ask you again. What do you want from me?

HANK: Damn it. I don't want nothin' from you.

[WALKER *shrugs and starts to walk away.*]

Walk away and be damned.

[WALKER *stops and turns back to* HANK.]

You know just what deal we been tryin' to make. [*He points at the platform.*] I'm askin' you to help me believe in him.

JOHNNY: I didn't know 'til this minute, brother, how truly evil you are. I see in your eyes that it ain't even possible for you to believe in him.

[HANK *laughs uproariously.*]

HANK: Right.

JOHNNY: Then why do you want to believe in him?

HANK: I'm askin' *you* to believe in him.[14]

From *Aria*:

SÁNÚ: You say. I have my scarab. [*In a narrative voice.*] Someone sent the Galisteo Public Library an annotated copy of Horace's Fourth Book of Odes. No one quite understood the point. After all, the two, perhaps three, troubadours active in the whole life of Galisteo had composed *rancheras*, wedding songs, *boleros*, *plenas*, *guajiras* and *sones de mariachi*, nothing remotely like those Roman artifices. At any rate, the book disappeared, to turn up in a Central Avenue pawnshop in Albuquerque, where it chummily sat festooned with ribbons and an exorbitant price. Leroy Baca offered an evening of authentic cockfighting in exchange for the text.[15]

14 *Selected Plays*, vol. 2, 123.
15 *Selected Plays*, vol. 1, 357.

From the *New York Times*, Saturday, August 9, 1975:

> Within two weeks, the whole town was sold. It was a dramatic change.
> Madrid, which once was a bustling coal town of 2,000 miners and their
> families, was reborn as a community.
>
> "From being lightfooted and not paying much rent, we've all become
> landholders with lots of responsibilities," said Diana Johnson, who with
> her husband, Mel, makes handblocked, printed clothes. The couple moved
> here from Chicago, where Mr. Johnson taught at the Art Institute nearly
> 20 years. They visualize Madrid, which is 50 miles north of Albuquerque
> and 30 miles south of Santa Fe, as a budding crafts center.

Walker and Hank argue: over the gun, over Hank's love for his wife,
Lily, and over the terms of their business agreement over Hank selling
in the park. They leave separately. Annie comes in, it's morning, and
she gives a monologue about how she is honest and can't simply let
go of, or even kill Hank, even if she wanted to. She exits. Morning.
Hank and Tommy enter. Hank has beaten Tommy, because Tommy
has told him that many of the clothes on the wagon were stolen during
the night. Annie enters, doesn't know anything. The crapshooters en-
ter with clothes clearly from the wagon, but also wearing armbands
that mark them as Pastor Ames's men. They go to the band-stage and
begin setting up. Dobie enters. He is supposed to have the wagon and
doesn't. Hank gets angrier.

> DOBIE: You're welcome to it. It's in the yard. I don't want nothin' to
> do with it. [*Angrily.*] And I'm through with you. He spoke to me and
> told me clearly, leave it alone.
>
> HANK: He? Spoke to you? Told you clearly what? What the hell you
> talkin' about?
>
> DOBIE: You ain't got no idea.
>
> [HANK *shakes him.*]
>
> HANK: Give me an idea.
>
> DOBIE: Me. He. I myself. The man. The spirit who was standin' there…
>
> […]

DOBIE: …It was early mornin', and cold, and foggy. I had a cup 'a coffee to take the chill off. Watchin' the wagon all the time. When I finished the coffee, I had to pee. So I eased over near the fence and peed… I zipped up and turned around. And there he was. There I was. My double. Standin' right by the wagon, lookin' at me. [*Violently.*] And I hadn't gone near that wagon. He, I was there all the time. No mistake it was me. I rubbed my eyes, I shook myself, I looked away and looked back. Whatever I did, he, I, the spirit didn't move, steady watchin' me all the time. And I knew it would be death for me to go near that wagon. I turned around, and I come right on here. [16]

"A lot of people who wanted to be done with the world can do it here, but it has become much more of an opportunity to come to something," said Mr. Conrad.

"We're setting up a whole new process of living," he said, "but at the same time we're like a suburban Los Angeles nightmare of what the world is going to be like—no government system, no maintenance for 20 years, you know, everything had broken down here. There's no system to fall back on except your own self-reliance."

"We've got water problems, sewer problems, all kinds of problems which instead of paying someone else to solve, we're doing it ourselves and learning a lot in the process."

Over and over again, the words "obligation" and "responsibilities" and such phrases as "self-reliance" and "mutual help" pop up in conversations here. And the notion that a community must be painstakingly built, selflessly, serves as a driving force for dozens of hammerers, patching and nailing old houses back together in preparation for winter.

Hank is stunned, almost unable to act, but seems to come up with a plan. Walker appears, singing:

> Last night, I prayed and I prayed
> I prayed all night long
> Ooh, I prayed and I prayed

16 Wright, *Selected Plays*, vol. 2, 130–131.

> Until I found the Lion
> Until I found the Lion
>
> [Chorus]
>
> Last night I cried and I cried
> I cried all night long
> Oh, I cried and I cried
> Until I found the Lion
> Until I found the Lion

Hank calls Walker over and asks him if he's still got the gun. He does, and he tells Hank that "it's not just in [his] service, and that's the thing." He then tells Hanks that being with him the evening before was like a second Baptism, the first being with Pastor Ames. He starts to back away and invites Hank to the rally.

> HANK: …What would I be doin' celebratin' a man who's never looked me in the eye?

Hank turns away, rushes to Tommy, Annie, and Dowbie, and yells at them for things to sell. He angrily jumps on the band-stage and begins destroying the placards and the stage set.

> JOHNNY: Hank!
>
> [*Hank turns toward him.*]
>
> HANK: At your service.
>
> [WALKER *pulls the gun and shoots* HANK.]
>
> JOHNNY: I *wanted* to believe in *you*.[17]

Santa Fe, February–March, 2022

17 Wright, *Selected Plays*, vol. 2, 134.

BLUES RESTRUCTURALISM

Jay Wright's *Homage to Anthony Braxton*

David Grubbs

My reading of history impels me to think that music, speech, and calculation (the measuring of time and event) have been the complex relationships in which human spirit, action, social and political relationships have been most gloriously exemplified. I realize that asserting this makes literary phenomena seem primary.... I should stop to say here that I include in the speech community all those practitioners of verbal art who are not normally included: the griot, the old Testament prophet, the ritual chanter, the fabulist, the legist, the chronicler, the preacher, even the mathematician. Quite a list, you say. What's left out? Why, nothing. Not even poetry.[1]

HOMAGE TO ANTHONY BRAXTON is the sole play among Jay Wright's newly published trove of performance works to be set in what's described as the present in a large urban area in the United States. In its subject matter, this comparatively naturalistic play echoes a number of poems from Wright's first collection, *The Homecoming Singer* (1971). Both *Homecoming* and *Homage* put front and center the church, baptism broadly considered, work and assorted hustles to make a living, and, as in the poem "The End of an Ethnic Dream," the lived aftermath of stepping away from playing music professionally. The status of "the present" in the play's stage directions is a curious, ambiguous one given that *Homage to Anthony Braxton* has yet to be presented onstage, and

1 Jay Wright, quoted in Charles H. Rowell, "'The Unraveling of the Egg': An Interview with Jay Wright." *Callaloo* 19, "Jay Wright: A Special Issue" (Autumn 1983): 3–15. doi: 10.2307/2930927.

its first-time publication in 2022 in *Figurations and Dedications: Selected Plays of Jay Wright, Volume 2* doesn't provide the reader with a date of composition. Stipulating that the action occurs in the present creates two possible linkages: between the time of writing and the events that the play depicts as well as between the play's events and the time of its performance. The former underscores the time-capsule quality of a heretofore unperformed text; the latter suggests that what transpires in the play can and should be made contemporaneous with its staging.

The two recently published volumes of Wright's selected plays—so much that has yet to be performed, but also so much of his life's labor that hadn't previously appeared in print—can't help but throw light and shadows and patterns figurative and abstract that make it possible to read his poetic oeuvre differently, the two bodies of work set in sympathetic vibration. Project editor Will Daddario dates *Homage to Anthony Braxton* to 1984. (The earliest of the batch is *The Crossing*, from 1973, which like *Homage to Anthony Braxton* stipulates an all-Black cast.) From the start, it's clear that *Homage* operates differently from the formal experimentation of later plays such as *Passage*, *The Playing Space*, *Lemma*, *Syntax*, and *Aria*; but even as its events unfold in a realistic manner, its characters' linguistic resources place it in a continuum with Wright's poetry. As per the quotation from Wright's 1983 *Callaloo* interview that appears as this essay's epigraph, they both belong to "the speech community" to which he accords an importance commensurate with that of "calculation (the measuring of time and event)" and music.

In *Homage to Anthony Braxton*, the first two characters to appear are the physically imposing Hank Huitt, 45 years of age, and Annie Lewis, ten years his junior. The play orbits around the two of them, a dyad of hustlers immemorial. From his first words, Hank sets a standard for the slangy bantering of which this play is made: "Annie, if times get any harder in this nappy swamp, a lean dog will have to sew his tail to his booty to keep from quiverin' to death."[2] Most everyone in

2 Wright, *Selected Plays*, vol. 2, 89.

this realm—this swamp inside an American city—aims for inspired locutions and splendid jive; wit of necessity advertises wits and arrives with sharpened edges often deployed at the expense of others. Trucking in such image-rich language, Hank quickly arrives at the heart of the matter: "I got a stone new hustle ought to skin a three-fanged rattler."[3] Whatever backstory there is for these two is sketched in the faintest of outlines: Hank has a bad heart; somewhere in his past he couldn't hack it on the bandstand.

In marches Johnny Walker, a short man full of energy, young enough to be Hank's son. Johnny works for the political candidate Reverend Benjamin Ames, "the Lion," widely discussed throughout; the question looms whether or not he will appear in the play. Johnny's task is to solicit one-dollar donations in support of Pastor Ames's campaign, for which donors in return receive a stuffed lion. There's little among these characters that doesn't immediately announce itself as transactional, with the reward for supporting the candidacy of one of the neighborhood's own being a stuffed creature that no one wants. Johnny and Hank set about trading insults, harsh ones that echo and gain intensity over the length of the play. Referring to Ames, the kindest thing that Hank musters is "[h]e at least got you faggots to douche before you hit the streets," while Johnny dismisses Hank as a "leftover tramp."[4] A point of comparison between these characters—a sore one, soon festering—materializes when Johnny refers to himself as a professional musician, a singer, and one who's still in the game. Hank gets Annie to fork over a couple of dollars, only to refuse to take the stuffed lions and instead catches Johnny off-guard, physically menacing him from the start.

Each character arrives with his or her own hustle. Dobie Thomas shows up pushing a cart, making a show of a mysterious errand that turns out to be the delivery of items for Ames's rally: a roll of cloth, a placard, an American flag. Hank halfheartedly tries to pimp Annie.

3 *Selected Plays*, vol. 2, 89.
4 *Selected Plays*, vol. 2, 91.

Talk of the upcoming political rally becomes the occasion for Hank to air his perennial concern, namely that someone's going to try to clean up the park: "Pretty soon the park will be off limits. They'll shut down the bars. Only thing that will be open is the churches and Ames's mouth."[5] When Tommy rolls up selling clothes, Hank has it in mind to start a hustle with him ("Wouldn't you like to deal big money just once, and get your hat?"),[6] proposing that they join forces with Dobie to use his cart and peddle clothes at Ames's rally, somehow wrangling the status of "the only, and the only legitimate, concession in the park tomorrow."[7] As characters enter and exit the stage competing teams are proposed; when Hank wanders off, Tommy suggests to Dobie that the two of them cut Hank out of the deal.

After night falls, Ames's man Johnny makes the mistake of reentering the park, only to be tricked by Tommy, who talks him into trying on a coat, then deftly pins his arms. Tommy uses this opportunity to pinch Johnny's pouch of money, which he splits three ways with Dobie and Annie. The theft isn't the last of Johnny's nighttime troubles among the park's regulars; two unnamed men playing dice harass him, questioning and mocking his Blackness, forcing him to take a bite of ribs and a slug of whiskey, with the whole thing turning increasingly sour and escalating to the verge of a fight when Hank reappears and steps in.

The play demonstrates how quickly alliances in the park form and dissolve. Annie and Hank are tight until they're not. Tommy and Hank are going into business together until they don't. Hank is relentlessly abusive to Johnny until he saves him from a fight in which the latter is outnumbered. Much of the mystery of the play has to do with the challenge—a challenge that as outsiders Johnny and the reader or audience member will share—of making sense of the network of allegiances already at play in the park. Who trusts whom? Who has whose back and for how long? Under what circumstances does this shift?

5 Wright, *Selected Plays*, vol. 2, 98.
6 *Selected Plays*, vol. 2, 100.
7 *Selected Plays*, vol. 2, 103.

Johnny has to be a canny reader; his on-the-fly sizing up of the situation, of the players and their various hustles, necessitates urgent parsing of the rich, improvisatory flows of language with which he's confronted and to which he must respond. The importance placed on originality and style in distinctive turns of phrase—together with the possibility of using that verbal dexterity for gain—recalls the essential resource that is language for the Irish peddlers in John Millington Synge's plays. In this central moment in the play in which Hank comes to Johnny's aid, is there a possibility of a pivot? Might they make common cause?

If there is, it's short-lived. Johnny soon accuses Hank—here playing the role of protector—of masterminding the robbery: "You didn't have the nerve to come on the scene yourself. You sent the woman to mark me and two mules to haul the gold."[8] Hank takes this opportunity to offer a deal: he'll do what he can to recover the money if Johnny secures Ames's approval for them to peddle clothing during the rally. Johnny can't seem to understand what Hank wants from him—is it only the concession for sales? The request strikes him as sufficiently meager to defy comprehension. But what Hank also wants is for Johnny to respect him, to trust him in matters having to do with the park, with all things local; he needs Johnny to acknowledge his authority, an authority that's in direct conflict with Pastor Ames. Johnny wavers.

In the morning, all is worse for wear. The evening's plans lie shattered. Tommy's clothes have been stolen overnight, as has Dobie's wagon. The two unnamed crapshooters that menaced Johnny show up wearing stolen clothes, and lo and behold they're now working for Ames. Dobie tells a ghostly tale of seeing his double in the middle of the night and has taken it as a sign to stay away from the wagon, to abandon the hustle. In the light of day, Johnny does an about-face and unexpectedly testifies to the respect that he's now decided is owed to Hank:

> I learned a lesson about priorities yesterday. I ain't puttin' in any claims
> for past actions and losses. Fact is, I thank you. Because now we

8 *Selected Plays*, vol. 2, 121.

understand each other. I been baptized, old man. I went in the water with you. Strange thing. It was the second time. The first time was with Benjamin Ames. When we came out of the water, I felt a tremor in his body that I didn't feel in yours. And he ain't asked me about my old gigs and failin's.[9]

But Johnny's revelation and his contrite, sincere speech matter little to Hank, who's eaten up with a different concern: what's he going to sell? The clock's ticking. Johnny's avowal of the connection and the communion between the two men—that, unlike with Ames, they can speak honestly of one another's "failin's," and that they have a kinship as people who aspired to make their mark as musicians—fails to register with Hank, who's apoplectic at missing out on the day's hustle, his chance to hawk some goods and make some dough. Hank goes on a rampage, jumping onto the platform where Ames is scheduled to speak; he rips the flag and destroys the placards and all the trappings of the political rally. To the surprise of all, Johnny pulls out a gun and shoots Hank, bewailing "I *wanted* to believe in *you.*" The play comes to a sudden, crashing halt in a thicooket of questions about Johnny's dramatic change of heart—and the subsequent reversal, in which he kills Hank—toward a man whom the evening prior he had dismissed as a "pimp, thief, con man, blackmailer, a ready rogue for all occasions."[10] It's as if Hank's setting foot on the bandstand was a capital crime.

✳ ✳ ✳

What can be said about the bold gesture that is the play's title, paying homage to an individual who goes unmentioned throughout? It's not immediately clear what about this work nominates it as an homage to the composer and musician Anthony Braxton. Braxton (b. 1945) has long cut a unique figure in American music, and in trying to account

9 Wright, *Selected Plays*, vol. 2, 133.
10 *Selected Plays*, vol. 2, 124.

for his presence in the title of the play it helps to think about what he has signified at different moments in his career. (For perspective, Jay Wright was born a decade before Braxton.) Anthony Braxton grew up on the south side of Chicago, and as a young person his fixation on music paralleled his interest in science; he loved the doo wop and rock and roll of Frankie Lymon and The Teenagers—Lymon being all of three years his senior—at the same time that he counted as a personal hero V-2 rocket developer Wernher von Braun.[11] By age eighteen Braxton had begun playing jazz with his slightly older friends Roscoe Mitchell and Jack DeJohnette, all three to become celebrated figures. After a single semester in college, and owing to his family's inability to afford tuition, Braxton joined the US Army. Like many Black artists of his generation, the military provided the opportunity for him to focus primarily on music and to spend an extended period outside of the United States. Braxton was first stationed for a year and a half in nearby Highland Park, Illinois, where he played with the Fifth Army Band: "It was an excellent group, some of the best musicians I ever played with, even though it was a very *racist* organization: I was only the second black person in it.... I was very much aware that I was not accepted: lockers turned upside down, 'Nigger Go Away' signs, all that kind of stuff."[12] From there he joined the Eighth Army Band and was stationed in South Korea, where he practiced up to ten hours per day and studied recordings—on headphones; his predilections found few sympathetic ears—including landmark releases of the day such as John Coltrane's *Ascension* and *A Love Supreme* and Albert Ayler's *Bells*. Returning to Chicago, he reconnected with Roscoe Mitchell, Leo Smith, and others, and in 1965 joined the AACM (Association for

11 See Graham Lock, *Forces in Motion: Anthony Braxton and the Meta-Reality of Creative Music* (Mineola, NY: Dover, 2018), 40. For an additional book-length investigation of Braxton's work, see also Ronald Radano, *New Musical Figurations: Anthony Braxton's Cultural Critique* (Chicago: University of Chicago Press, 2009).

12 Lock, *Forces in Motion*, 45.

the Advancement of Creative Musicians),[13] the collective that would eventually be recognized as a who's who of many of the most important musical artists of the last half century: Muhal Richard Abrams, Roscoe Mitchell, Joseph Jarman, Lester Bowie, Wadada Leo Smith, Leroy Jenkins, George Lewis, Amina Claudine Myers, and Henry Threadgill, among others.

In addition to his own brilliant playing, Braxton's music came to be known for embracing extremes of scale. In 1969 he recorded *For Alto*, one of the first full albums of solo reed recordings, released in 1971 as a double LP by Chicago's Delmark Records. Braxton's profile grew through his time with Chick Corea, Dave Holland, and Barry Altschul in the quartet Circle, and in 1975 he began a six-year run of albums under his own name for the major label Arista, an opportunity that Braxton met ambitiously with everything from another solo alto recording (*Alto Saxophone Improvisations 1979*) to the twenty-two piece ensemble of *Creative Orchestra Music 1976* (it's worth noting that the titles of its six pieces appear on the sleeve as diagrams consisting of geometric figures, dashed lines, and numbers, along with what one assumes to be the major-label compromise nomenclature "Cut One," "Cut Two," etc.) to *Composition No. 95 for Two Pianos* (his final release for Arista

13 For histories of the AACM, see George E. Lewis, *A Power Stronger than Itself: The AACM and American Experimental Music* (Chicago: University of Chicago Press, 2008) and Paul Steinbeck, *Sound Experiments: The Music of the AACM* (Chicago: University of Chicago Press, 2022), as well as two related essays by Lewis about Black American musicians and their European counterparts: "Improvised Music after 1950: Afrological and Eurological Perspectives," *Black Music Research Journal* 16:1 (Spring, 1996): 91–122, and "Gittin' to Know Y'all: Improvised Music, Interculturalism, and the Racial Imagination," *Critical Studies in Improvisation* 1:1 (2004). For an overview of the AACM's best-known group, the Art Ensemble of Chicago, including encounters with Anthony Braxton in Chicago and abroad, see Paul Steinbeck, *Message to Our Folks: The Art Ensemble of Chicago* (Chicago: University of Chicago Press, 2017).

in 1982) and the 1978 triple-LP boxed set *For Four Orchestras* (nearly two hours of music performed by 156 musicians from Oberlin College's Conservatory of Music and presented in quadraphonic sound). Among other awards, Braxton has been honored with a MacArthur Fellowship, a Guggenheim Fellowship, an NEA Jazz Master Award, and a United States Artists Fellowship. Having recently marked his 75th birthday, his work still encompasses large-scale projects (including his *Trillium* operas, a projected cycle of twelve works) as well as performances in a range of duo pairings and smaller ensembles.

The first things that Anthony Braxton signifies in a world in which one might encounter Jay Wright's *Homage to Anthony Braxton* are that he's a musician, a successful one, and a Black artist raised in one of America's most segregated cities. Braxton's renown marks the distance between himself and the characters Hank and Johnny, both of whom are introduced early in the play as failed musicians, those who made a go of it and have nothing to show for it save bantering recollections or, in the case of Johnny, a dimming if not yet extinguished ambition to make it as a singer. The action in *Homage to Anthony Braxton* takes place before the play's stage-within-a-stage, the bandstand that beckons to but welcomes neither Hank nor Johnny, and which on the occasion of Hank's trespass marks the site of the shooting that rings down the end of the play.

Anthony Braxton hovers above the play as an example of a fully realized artist that neither of these main characters will become. But there are also hints of how his biography intersects with—could be imagined as crossing paths with, however fleetingly—the character Johnny Walker. Johnny's experience as a singer dates from his time in the military. Like Braxton, he spent time as a young Black American abroad navigating an unfamiliar milieu; other characters in the play—the park's regulars—view his time outside of the US as cause for suspicion. In Braxton's case, the high profile that he has enjoyed in Europe has been cause for a similar sort of suspicion from traditionalist American critics that his music is insufficiently rooted in the jazz tradition. Braxton frequently references the "trans-idiomatic" as a central aspect of his work, not only as a musician and composer, but also as a teacher, and in his writings and interviews, where he often seems as likely to refer to Richard Wagner or Karlheinz Stockhausen as he is to discuss Duke Ellington or Charlie Parker.

When the two unnamed craps players in *Homage to Anthony Braxton* harass Johnny, one of the things they accuse him of is being a narc. Johnny sings a bit of blues, to which one remarks, "Naw, I think you're a narco bull. You don't have that soul sound."[14] There's no escaping critics. When Johnny initially turns down a bite of ribs and sip of whiskey, the first dice player comes out and says it: "[O]ut here in this dark, I can't even tell if you're black or not. Have you ever seen a blood look like him? . . . Have you ever heard of a blood who'd turn down some ribs and a taste?"[15] After Hank saves Johnny from the two-on-one fight—with the accusation of Johnny's singing not having soul still freshly stinging—the exchange that follows is the longest in the play to touch on music and performance:

HANK: . . . Just where did you do this professional thing of yours?

JOHNNY: All over. France, England, up north, Japan, Hawaii.

HANK: I'll bet you didn't do but two weeks in the cotton belt. Now, did you?

[WALKER *turns on him slowly.*]

JOHNNY: Four. But I was in Europe. I played the military service clubs through England, France, Germany. Got a couple of gigs out of it up in Denmark and Sweden. I wanted to stay there and just gig from then on, but, you know, the novelty wears off. Things don't come up. You can't make it. I thought I was in on a package tour. [*He stops, looks up toward where the two men were.*] Hard to convince the deaf. Anyway, I ain't into that anymore.[16]

---

14 Wright, *Selected Plays*, vol. 2, 116.
15 *Selected Plays*, vol. 2, 118.
16 *Selected Plays*, vol. 2, 120–122.

Like seemingly everyone else in the park, Hank can't help but get a dig in about Johnny's lack of Black bona fides: "I'll bet you didn't do but two weeks in the cotton belt."

If playing abroad during his military service had marked the end of Braxton's career as a performer—and think of how many souls whose careers did end there—his story might not have been so dissimilar. But even with Braxton's success—and to no small extent because of Braxton's success—his career has been dotted by the sorts of insults that Johnny weathers, namely as someone whose music, and particularly when Braxton began to be recognized as a composer as well as a performer, lacks roots in Black vernacular music. Braxton has addressed this at length:

> In my opinion, I believe my work, for whatever reason, in some way, has, I am viewed as the Negro who has gone outside of the categories assigned to me. My work was not idio-centric, in a way, where I could be of value to the forces, which are rebuilding components in this time period. This is true for the African-American antebellum traditionalist's sentiments who have always mistrusted me and I can respect that. But at the same time, we're talking now about an effort that is thirty-five to forty years and the isolation that I have experienced is not unique when I think of the great work of Leroy Jenkins, the great work of Henry Threadgill, the great work of Connie Crothers. So, no, the jazz people couldn't use a guy like me…. It is not the kind of thing that the jazz structure is prepared to deal with. If I would say, "Swing baby, swing and burn it up," then there would be room for a guy like me.[17]

In the same interview, Braxton names the critics Albert Murray and Stanley Crouch as "the Lincoln Center sector" traditionalists who dismissed him on the basis that "Oh, well, he doesn't play the blues"—an observation Braxton argues amounts to a fundamental misunderstanding of the blues.

17 Fred Jung, "A Fireside Chat with Anthony Braxton," Jazzweekly.com, 2022, http://www.jazzweekly.com/interviews/abraxton.htm.

Johnny faces similar sorts of judgment in the play, particularly having to do with a perceived lack of feeling for the blues. What a thing for a singer to hear! The accusations that Johnny faces come from *Homage to Anthony Braxton*'s only unnamed characters, seemingly occupying the lowest rank within the social organization of the park until they roll up the next morning with freshly lifted clothes and a job working for Reverend Ames. By contrast, some of the most pointed criticism that Braxton has endured came from prominent Black critics associated in the late 1980s and 1990s with Jazz at Lincoln Center, individuals Braxton saw as trying to separate his work from what they regarded as the most meaningful, valuable jazz lineage, instead relegating him to a neither-nor world of experimentalism, one that whatever it was above all wasn't Black.

Braxton's longtime colleague George Lewis shares in much of the credit for pushing back against a narrow, sclerotic defining not only of jazz tradition, but also of what should be understood as belonging to a tradition of American experimental music. Like Braxton, Lewis has been an AACM member; he's also a trombonist who has performed with Braxton in numerous settings including Braxton's *Creative Orchestra Music 1976* album, and like Braxton, he's an exemplary trans-idiomatic composer and trailblazing Black artist who has worked toward the transformation of the largely White sphere of music and academia.[18]

Accusations of not being able to play the blues have been painful to Braxton. In conversation with biographer Graham Lock, he points out "People say I don't play the blues—I've always played the blues,

18 See Lewis. *A Power Stronger than Itself* is many things; not only is it a detailed history of the AACM's coming into existence and its many achievements, but it also functions as a series of interlinking short biographies, gently interrupting the book's chronology to leap back generations whenever an important player enters the scene, so that we understand these individuals not only through their musical training as younger people, but also through the history of their families. It's an exceptional book about the south side of Chicago, but it's also about Black rural-to-urban internal migration in the twentieth century.

but I never argue about those kinds of things. What we call the blues is not just notes, it's a vibrational understanding that been transmitted and encoded, and it's manifested in various forms of music in various different ways." When Lock asks Braxton where blues fits in with his notion of historical cycles of "restructuralism, stylism, and traditionalism," Braxton objects to the idea of blues, even in the present, as being traditionalist: "No sir! Everything goes forward—there's a restructured blues."[19]

✴ ✴ ✴

In "Wednesday Night Prayer Meeting," the first poem in *The Homecoming Singer*, there's a split-screen juxtaposition between "the boys and girls…come in / from their flirting game of tag, / with the prayers they've memorized, / the hymns they have even to start" and "[o]utside, the pagan kids /…kissing each other with a shy humility, / or urinating boldly against the trees."[20] It's as if the kids pissing on trees are still doing so however many years later in *Homage to Anthony Braxton*; with adulthood, the divide is ever starker. As Hank sermonizes, making his case for the truths of the park:

> What can he, the Reverend Benjamin Ames, tell you that the unholy Henry the Hank Huitt can't? That you have been given the burden of wearin' the thorny crown of your skin? That you will never be free? That you can only be free? I been studyin' it. [*He holds up his hand.*] Prophecy. The end of the world will not come. No one will lose. But the only winners will be those who know how to move on without runnin' away. You see what I'm sayin'. There is no way out.[21]

To this, Tommy gives him something like an amen: "That is definitely hard, my man." Hank is one of those souls described in "Wednesday Night Prayer Meeting" who "have closed their night with what certainty

19 Lock, *Forces in Motion*, 166.
20 Jay Wright, "Wednesday Night Prayer Meeting," *Transfigurations: Collected Poems* (Baton Rouge, LA: Louisiana State Univ. Press, 2000), 3.
21 Wright, *Selected Plays*, vol. 2, 103.

they could unwilling to exchange their freedom for a god."[22] Outside of the church, many of the poems in *The Homecoming Singer* center on work: the cannery, house painting, and so on. The individuals depicted in these poems are up early. If the characters in *Homage to Anthony Braxton* aren't working regular hours—they don't have bosses, at least not in name—they're certainly working late and getting up early, once again demonstrating how much work it is to be poor in America.

The continuities among Wright's poetry and his newly revealed plays—or in this instance the continuities among his poetry and the verbal inventions of the park's occupants in *Homage to Anthony Braxton*—make it difficult, even counterproductive to think of these practices as especially distinct from one another. One keeps returning to Wright's term "the community of speech." But remember that along with speech and calculation Wright places music among "the complex relationships in which human spirit, action, social and political relationships have been most gloriously exemplified."[23]

Squint and you can see the many feints and twists in one of Anthony Braxton's long melodic lines in Wright's verse as long, line-broken sentences enjamb their way down the page. This is also homage. Wright himself is a bass player, but one who set it aside, at least professionally, if we are to take "The End of an Ethnic Dream" as autobiography:

> My bass a fine piece of furniture.
> My fingers soft, too soft to rattle
> rafters in second-rate halls.
> The harmonies I could never learn
> stick in Ayler's screams.[24]

22 Wright, *Transfigurations*, 6.
23 Quoted in Rowell, "Unraveling of the Egg."
24 *Transfigurations*, 20.

COLLECTIVE SILENCE IN *THE DELIGHTS OF MEMORY*

Michael Paul Berlin

THE DELIGHTS OF MEMORY, a play in five parts, is the product of a period of publishing silence in Jay Wright's career. Following his winning of a MacArthur "Genius Grant" in 1987, Wright published only *Elaine's Book* (1988) and *Boleros* (1991), before his next publication of new work of poetry, *Music's Mask and Measure*, sixteen years later. Movements of *The Delights of Memory* were published during this time and part one, titled "Lilly," was performed in 1994. Within the body of Wright's work, this challenging series of plays amplifies the silence that permeate his work as a whole. Like his poetic work, this cycle of plays is invested in aesthetic force of what cannot be said or held in common. More than in his poetry, silence finds its measure against what must be said, but cannot yet be understood. Its primary tension is that of working through the nexus of familial and societal trauma in taught scenes of interracial and intergenerational confrontation.

All of the vignettes that constitute *The Delights of Memory* play out between September and October 1963, the months leading up to the Kennedy Assassination. However, we get the sense from reading these plays that the Mesa, Arizona in which they occur is a place where the grand sweep of America's official history is felt less distinctly, as its inequities are lived more profoundly. For a poet so invested in the concept of history—private, public, and universal—Wright's foregrounding of memory in this cycle of plays offers his readers a different point of entry to his work. Wright had explored the powers of memory in the poem "The Charge," from *Soothsayers and Omens* (1976), in which he wrote:

> Now, father
> I am more than yours,
> and lead you past the tricks
> of our memory, into this moment,
> as real as memory.
> This is the moment
> when all our unwelcome deaths
> charge us to be free.[1]

There is an intimacy in memory for Wright that for all of its "tricks" demands reckoning in the present. On the borderland between the global rhythm of Wright's poetry and death, memory implies a community rooted somewhere in between privation and redemption.

The cycle of plays that constitute *The Delights of Memory* is concerned with the fate of a single Black family, the Porters, as they subsist and work with the weight of their interlocking pasts. The first, second, and fourth plays of this cycle consist of a counterpoint between members of the family and white interlocutors; the third play consists of a dramatic monologue, while the fifth brings together the Porter family in an uneasy polyphony. As the characters enter moments of union and disunion, the action of each vignette hangs on the precipice of an atonement that remains just out of the characters' reach. These failures resound with the weight of both private and historical memory.

The tensions that divide the Porter family reach a crescendo in the last play of the cycle, "Awaking and Forgetting." In this play, Lilly and Doss Porter, the heads of this family, reach an impasse on the relationship between Christian revelation and political reflection. Drawing from W.E.B. Du Bois's *Black Reconstruction*, Doss tells his piously Christian

---

1 Wright, "The Charge," in *Soothsayers and Omens* (New York: Seven Woods Press, 1976).

wife that, "Foolish talk, all of this, you say, of course; and that is because no American now believes in his religion. Its facts are mere symbolism; its revelations vague generalities…"[2] Remaining with the passing joy of emancipation, Doss stresses its emotional exuberance "A great human sob shrieked in the wind, and tossed its tears upon the sea—free, free, free." In doing so, he condemns his wife for her continued desire to believe in something like redemption that would remove them from what he calls "a gnat's nest of a town." Their search for more than the "vague generalities" of a moral arch becomes tragic in their failure to find meaning in each other's yearnings.

This effort to find a way forward, as a family, forms the action of the play that opens the cycle, "Lilly," in which the titular character confronts a white bank guard, Jim Tompkins, about their shared history. Denying any knowledge of her, at first, and of the death, or disappearance, of a man named Will Lewis, as time goes on, Tompkins represents the unspoken norms that stratify the closed off community in which the plays occur. Tompkins's silences and disavowals evince a tacit authority that Lilly confronts him with when she tells Tompkins that she passes "by the bank, and I see you, starchy clean, lookin like the law."[3] To this observation, Lilly quickly adds: "Or should I say, that law? [*Pause.*] But you'll answer to the other one, Jim Tompkins. I'll see to that." The displacement of the law opened up by these lines instantiates an interrogation of the boundaries between public and private life and forms of justice that are possible in each sphere. This division follows closely upon that between divine justice and that which can be obtained in the temporal sphere.

This sense of displacement leads finally to an act of expiation. Purifying her garden as a site of both subsistence and resistance, Lilly picks "up the glass of water, and slowly sprinkles the water, drop by drop, in a circle, as the lights close on her beatific smile."[4] Representing, also,

2 Wright, *Selected Plays*, vol. 2, 341.
3 *Selected Plays*, vol. 2, 237.
4 *Selected Plays*, vol. 2, 252.

an offering to the dead this silent gesture bridges past and present in an act of working through. From the matriarch of the family the next play moves on to the father, Doss Porter. The most straightforwardly dramatic of the vignettes that comprise *The Delights of Memory*, "Doss" builds tensions between its titular character and Brad Manning, a white man who wants to hire Doss as a cook on his train, which culminates in an inversion of text and subtext, resounding with violence.

Naming, which J. Peter Moore recently identified as central to Wright's poetics, forms a primary point of tension and control in "Doss."[5] The violence that Manning ends up visiting upon Doss brings to the fore not only the forms of unfreedom that attend the history of race in the United States but also those of class. Like Tompkins, Manning becomes a fleeting source of authority in the text. At the play's opening, Manning asserts his power by insisting on calling Doss, Dawson. In using Doss's "government name," Manning authors his agency over his subject and sets the stage for his interview as an interrogation aimed at unearthing his potential employee's "authentic" past. Manning's insistence on discovering the truth of this history assumes a more insidious dimension, as he claims greater mastery over its particulars than Doss. Pointing out discrepancies in Doss's record, Manning exclaims: "Don't be ridiculous, Doss. Take those things to their logical conclusion, you don't even exist, and I could be talkin to a ghost."[6] Denigrating Doss as merely spectral, Manning renders him as a nonentity outside of his potential to work.

The conflict between the characters comes to a climax when Manning physically threatens Doss. Diffusing the situation by offering to share a drink with Manning, Doss inadvertently opens a locker on the train which reveals "a Klan white hood, a hangman's noose, pamphlets and a gun." Seizing the gun, Doss sets in motion the rest of the cycle's dramatic

5 See J. Peter Moore, "Rhythm, Divination, and Naming in Jay Wright's Poetry," *Hyperallergic*, January 4, 2020, https://hyperallergic.com/524557/the-prime-anniversary-jay-wright/.

6 Wright, *Selected Plays*, vol. 2, 266.

action at the vignette's end. The next play in the series, "Leroy," breaks the silences that fall over the rest of the play with an extended soliloquy, delivered by one of the Porters' two sons, Leroy. The brashness of Leroy's speech accentuates its status as the only non-dialogic portion of the cycle. It is difficult to tarry with the raw verism with which Wright paints Leroy's unalloyed invective. Yet, between his violent projections, we find that it is Leroy who sees clearest into the white supremacy within which the Porters find themselves surrounded. More than Doss or his adopted brother, David, it is also Leroy who directly experiences the brunt of Klan brutality. Recalling an attack against a Black family on whose land gold was found, Leroy recalls:

> And there in my face was a burnin cross, man. A burnin cross. On Ike
> Napoleon's land. Talk about confusion. I felt fiery, and I wanted to shout.
> But I couldn't make a sound. I was gaggin like a man with a heart attack.
> And I started to run toward the cross, beatin my fists in the air.[7]

In this dialectic of speech and silence, Leroy's mute gestures accentuate the horror of what he has witnessed. Its traumatic effect is registered by his observation "But sometimes the wrong memory can drain happiness from your heart." A moment lost to the course of history, what Leroy observes belongs to the realm of fantasy and loss. Unrecuperable, Leroy's pain finds purchase in his attacks on his brother.

David is at once the most relatable and most distant character in the play. We find in the course of his dialogue with the character Barney Jacobs that he is reading a book titled, "African Worlds: Studies in the Cosmological Ideas and Social Values of African Peoples." Attacked for his intellectual curiosity by both Jacobs and Leroy, David's engagement with the world comes nearest to closing the distance that exists between characters. This monadic spacing and proximity between characters and their dialogue is evocative of a work like W.H. Auden's *Age of Anxiety*. Like this work, the characters of *The Delights of Memory* approach a pervasive sense of catastrophe that they cannot fully name.

7 *Selected Plays*, vol. 2, 288–289.

Familiar from Wright's poetry, this apophasis, or the rhetoric and theological technique of defining something via negative relief, points to something greater than the characters that unites them in their differences and propels them forward to a collective fate.

This coming apart, together, serves as the architecture for the cycle's last play. In this prolonged scene, the events set in motion when Doss seizes Manning's gun come to their grim conclusion. The ending, however, is almost beside the point. It is rather the sense of inexorability that gives this vignette its resonance. We have had the foresense throughout the cycle that the characters of this cycle would escape neither the hermetic seal of Mesa nor the pain that recognition brings. Rather than ending in reversal, this recognition empties into the silence that punctuates the play. As David says to his mother: "I had made your heart as respectful of silence as I wanted to be."[8] The silencing to which members of this family have subjected themselves remains, at last, a function of their nearness. It becomes a form of love inverted in its intensity. The characters of this play demand more of each other than they can possibly give.

If a sense of ineffability is definitive of Wright's poetry, then this dramatic attention to the devastating effects of silence enacts the violence that his poems defer to the margins. Whereas Wright's poetry dwells on what cannot be said, this drama confronts us with what must be said against the indifference of a world that would silence it. One of the play's last sounds, a scream, juts out from under the closure enacted by the mysterious figure who leads the characters away to what can be read as either their judgment or martyrdom. It is the ephemerality of performance that makes the final disappearance of the characters all the more haunting. Far from the thrall of national tragedy, the Porters' ending occupies the sacred space of private recollection. Cutting as the title's irony is, it points to the urgent work, in a nation unable to awake from its past, of summoning the dead.

8 Wright, *Selected Plays*, vol. 2, 350.

NO REDEMPTION

Fate and Limbo in The Delights of Memory

Esteban Rodríguez

FOR THOSE FAMILIAR with Catholicism, the concept of Purgatory serves to purify the recently deceased who courted God's friendship and favor during their lifetimes, yet still need their souls to be cleansed to enjoy the full array of heaven's offerings. In popular imagination, Purgatory is thought to be a place, one that, although it might not have the fire and damnation of hell, is ripe with some degree of suffering. The Catholic Church, however, never mentions it as a physical space; rather it is one of existence, a process that seeks to purify a troubled soul until it reaches holiness. Whatever way one thinks of Purgatory, it does add some gray to what is generally a black and white Christian concept of sin, death, and the afterlife. It also offers hope to believers that heaven is attainable, that there is a path that will lead to eternal happiness.

For readers of Jay Wright's poetry, there might be a sense of entering a purgatorial space the moment they dive into the page, especially with regards to some of his most demanding works, like *The Dimensions of History* (1976) and *The Double Invention of Komo* (1980). This is not to say that when entering the realm of Wright's verse readers are entering a place where they feel guilt for their past, but they do enter a particular type of limbo, one more colloquial than doctrinal, and there is always a distinct possibility that at the end of a poem, questions will be much more abundant than answers.

While Wright's dramas no doubt have more of a skeleton to them than the poems (as all plays must), there is still a unique quality to each that demands a certain amount of cultural knowledge that is not given to readers outright. There must be a reading in between the lines, sometimes even for basic interpretation, and *The Delights of Memory*, a multiple part drama with a cast of characters attempting to come to grips with a past they might not fully remember, no doubt requires connecting dots to uncover more sinister truths.

The Delights of Memory, to summarize briefly, centers on Lily Porter, Dawson "Doss" Porter, Leroy Porter, and David Murphy (who has been taken in by the Porters) as they navigate encounters where a shared and often haunting past slowly unravels, surprising and shocking them moment after moment. Lily Porter, in "Lily," the first part of *Delights*, confronts Jim Tompkins one afternoon about his role in the death of Will Lewis, a role that Tompkins doesn't remember and yet which he becomes increasingly agitated by the more Lily presses him to admit his responsibility. Doss Porter's meeting with Bradley Manning in part two, "Doss," lacks the surreal and mysterious quality found in "Lily," but the suspense that steadily builds unearths the real reasons Doss passes on working for Manning. In part three, "Leroy," the title character's demons return to haunt him in a monologue where he admits that he must be "losin [his] mind," and in "David," part four, David Murphy's contentious conversation with Barney Jacobs yields more than just adolescent questions of friendship, race, intelligence, history, and the nature of being confined by one's surroundings. This all leads to the fifth and final part, "Awaking and Forgetting," where the characters confront each other in a chaotic and unapologetic manner that ultimately renders the appearance of a figure that will take them across the river and into an "awakening [they] might want to forget." (It should be noted that although Lily isn't led by this figure outside their home, she does meet a fate that has her screaming.) But before we arrive at this climactic ending, we witness a purgatorial sense of loss, regret, and a desire to escape the realities and actions of a past that brought each character to their present moment.

By all accounts, Lily Porter is the only character whose attempts to atone for her sins makes her a suitable candidate to exit the purgatory of Mesa City and be welcomed by the open arms of heaven, applauded for her insistence that all wrongs can be made right. Her trajectory toward this limbo isn't described or discussed in detail throughout the play, and there are only fragments that surface in the first and last parts. But she does undergo a journey, and given what she faces toward the end, it isn't a stretch to see her journey as at least partly similar to that of the pilgrim Dante in *The Divine Comedy* who travels through the confines and labyrinths of Hell. (In fact, many of Wright's plays involve if not a physical journey through personal purgatories, then at least an emotional and mental one filled with hauntings, horrors, and an honest assessment of the horrible future that awaits.) But unlike Dante, Lily doesn't descend to learn how to achieve true salvation; rather, her actions have put her there, and by the play's conclusion, despite her seeming to reach the surface of purgatory a slightly changed person, she meets a brutal end. Her screaming was merely a prologue to the greater suffering that would ensue, and as such, we are led to question to what extent redemption is attainable. If we return to the Catholic notion of Purgatory, we must believe righteousness is always within our reach, especially after recognizing and accepting our shortcomings and giving ourselves fully to the authority of God.

But even though purgatory (again, in the more colloquial sense) is rampant throughout *The Delights of Memory*, no one is worthy of moving beyond their past actions and entering a different conclusion (this always appears to be the case in Dante's *Inferno* and *Purgatorio*, since what Dante is witnessing, even while immersing himself in the scenarios presented, is merely the consequences of the actions one took). In this particular world Wright has created, there is no redemption. There are redemptive qualities that the characters no doubt embody and enact, but total redemption, and therefore eternal happiness, always remains out of reach.

Looking at Lily Porter more closely, we see a woman who wants nothing more than for others to come to the truth. In the first section, Lily finds herself face to face with Jim Tompkins, a banker whose past

Lily uncovers the longer their conversation plays out. Tompkins keeps denying his role, saying that he has no idea what Lily is speaking about (although it could be interpreted that now that he is in this state of purgatory, he's lost all recollection of his past life), and even when pressed with specifics, he abstains from any wrongdoing. Tompkins's oscillation between utter confusion and being fully aware that he knows everything that happened in the past creates a tension that Lily attempts to dissect, pushing and pushing until snippets of a violent encounter reveal themselves. What truly creates the suspense here is the fact that Jim's anger is never on full display; rather it builds precisely because he toggles between feelings he is trying to process more fully, and with Lily's persistence, we see Tompkins confess enough to reveal his guilt:

> PORTER: Then he didn't even tell you the question that would lead to the secret. [*She nods knowingly.*] I see. And for that you shot him.
>
> TOMPKINS: [*Almost now in utter anguish.*] I did not shoot him. I lost him just the way you did.
>
> PORTER: What did you say to him when he got in the truck?
>
> TOMPKINS: I don't remember.
>
> PORTER: [*Skeptically.*] Don't remember. Somethin that important and you don't remember. I would never have forgotten. [*Abruptly.*] Why do you think I've been after you? I want to hear his last words.
>
> TOMPKINS: There were no last words.
>
> PORTER: You didn't speak?
>
> TOMPKINS: We spoke.
>
> PORTER: What did he say? What did you do?
>
> TOMPKINS: I might have told him what others were sayin.
>
> PORTER: What did they say?
>
> TOMPKINS: Nothin it would do any good for you to hear. Not now, anyway. It's all over. [*He turns agitatedly away from her.*] I'm glad really that you pursued me. [*He turns to her, and edges into pleading.*] You see,

it gives me an opportunity to say that it doesn't matter what was said, what was done. I'm not that man anymore. [*He shows her his uniform.*] You can see I'm not dressed for the fields, and my fingers don't have the smell of that special juice the earth gives. [*He drops his arms.*] All things have changed. I've even forgiven you.

PORTER: For what? You are confused. I came to put myself in the way of healin, to see if I could forgive you. [*She fingers the beans.*] That's why I'm never without these. So that, when we meet, as we do now, you might hear the spirit chatterin and realize how close we came to bein inseparable. That's why you were waitin in the truck, and that's why I didn't go out to beat you away from Will. I was testin my strength and his love, and I made a mistake. [*Pause. She looks slowly at him.*] Who should pay, Jim Tompkins? I'm not so sure now. Are you?[1]

While there is never an outright admission, there is still a confession, but more surprisingly are Lily's past actions, or rather inactions, in relation to Jim's. To sit back and watch as Jim ended Will's life merely to test her strength of love for Will is not only religiously unconscionable, but humanly unjust, and Lily recognizes this fully, albeit too late. No one can truly predict their reactions to a life-threatening situation, especially when they are witnesses to it. But knowing that you can change the trajectory of someone's future, or at least steer it enough so the outcome isn't complete non-existence shouldn't objectively be as complicated as Lily experienced it. Regardless of what was or wasn't racing through Lily's mind, she must reckon with the consequences, but like a child who only realizes they did something wrong after the fact, Lily embodies the exact same attitude, and more than anything we see a selfishness that finally comes to light. Jim Tompkins places the onus back on Lily, and throughout this interaction, we see Lily's tone and demeanor alternate between subtle righteousness and guilt. At times, it doesn't even appear as though she is talking to Jim, but rather to herself (imagine her gazing past Jim or into the audience, a look of determination with hues of defeat smeared across her face).

1 Wright, *Selected Plays*, vol. 2, 246–247.

Perhaps she knows that even if Jim were to recognize his past actions, a good part of them wouldn't change, which is why when she poses the question at the end of their exchange in "Lily," she knows she is truly asking herself who is to blame and who should pay. The lack of a concrete response that follows is quite deafening, and it is perhaps at this point that we truly see there will be no resolution.

Nevertheless, several questions arise throughout the exchange above: Why does Jim Tompkins suddenly feel that he can forgive Lily? What exactly does Lily mean about "bein inseparable"? Who does Lily believe should pay for Will's death if not Jim? If not her? There are no immediate or concrete answers, but there is a clear narrative that emerges: Lily sacrificed someone else's life to enrich hers, and in the process, she lost the opportunity to be pure (or however pure one can truly be in this world).

This selfishness, however, doesn't reside in their heart forever, and in "Awaking and Forgetting," we find Lily attempting to let Doss know that he too can seek forgiveness and come to terms with the past:

> Doss, you don't have to apologize to me. After all, I left my sins in the water, too. It's not up to me to forgive you. And, though it may be a sin to say so, I do forgive you. There is nothin' that you have to face that I won't go there with you. Ever.[2]

Here, Lily sounds more like a mother than anything that resembles a partner, and although she is uncertain about her path to righteousness, she's certain that she can find peace because she has come to terms with everything that she is and isn't:

> A note from Jim Tompkins. He calls me a witch, not a holy woman. The rest you can see for yourself. Lies and promises he can never keep. I will not die. I will not disappear. I will not cease to witness to the spirit within me.[3]

Lily recognizes who she truly is, and in turn has allowed forgiveness to enter her heart. There is a relief that while not physically visible, at least to the audience, is emotionally prominent. We can see her acceptance

2 Wright, *Selected Plays*, vol. 2, 343–344.
3 *Selected Plays*, vol. 2, 373.

manifest in the tone of her voice, and this is perhaps why she feels confident when she steps out of her house to meet her friend Amy Hargrove (although, given that moments later we hear "two women's voices scream," it's safe to say that Lily wasn't granted the full redemption she believed she was going to receive). This forgiveness, however, is by no means contagious, and even though the discussion here is meant to ease the tension Doss is feeling toward Lily, as well as his perceived slights by other people in his past, Doss is anything but receptive. In the final section, Doss and Lily are discussing the events that occurred the night they were with Jim Tompkins and Will Lewis, and despite the tangents with David and Leroy about their role in the community, as well as within the religious/spiritual realm, Doss remains unchanged, unwilling to accept anything short of his own desires:

> [*With a touch of irony.*] Foolish talk. The doors are locked. The neighborhood's buzzin with buzzards. I can see the lights in every other house slowly goin' out. And at every window there's a shadow, and a face turned toward me. What did I do to these people that they'll deny me my power?[4]

Doss's main concern is power he believes he is owed—power of influence, of respect, of fear. Doss is not necessarily in the wrong here. In many ways, the scene here, to use *The Divine Comedy* as a guide again, almost appears to resemble Virgil and Dante's entrance through the gates of the City of Dis in the *Inferno*, and we can view the same emotion that overtakes Doss present in Virgil:

> Our adversaries slammed the heavy gates
>> in my lord's face, and he stood there outside,
>> then turned slowly toward me and walked back very slowly
>
> with eyes downcast, all self-assurance now
>> erased from his forehead—sighing, "Who are these
>> to forbid my entrance to the halls of grief!"[5]

4 *Selected Plays*, vol. 2, 374.
5 Dante Alighieri, *Inferno*, trans. Mark Musa (New York: Penguin, 1984), 142.

Doss, however, is no Virgil (he has no intention of helping anyone but himself), and as his interactions with Bradley Manning demonstrate, he is seen as someone that others can take advantage of. Still, there is a fine line between acceptance and power, and while there is no doubt that he has been accepted (as a cook, as a man, as a member of Mesa City) by the larger community, he doesn't have either their respect or fear. He himself is full of fear, and we see this in his final act. When Lily steps outside to meet her friend, Doss "picks up the pistol and moves quickly to her side, looking toward the yard." There is no indication that Doss has been outright ostracized by the community, but there is no indication either that he has won over their good graces. He is terrified that his neighbors have come to feed on his rotting soul, and when confronted with the figure, the anger that was swelling in him, and that had perhaps been for years, quickly subsides, since he knows his end is near. T.S. Eliot might have said that the world will end with a whimper and not a bang, but for anyone who comes face to face with death as a result of their actions, a violence will always be present, and it will serve as that last reminder of the fate one creates during their lifetime.

One question that should be asked is why Lily and Doss have remained in this limbo for so long. What keeps their souls still tethered to Mesa City? Purgatory is meant as a process of purification, for the elect to achieve holiness before their ascent to heaven. But what if their process hasn't been fully realized, if their recognition of who they were and what they had done through these five acts was merely that, a recognition? Instead of heaven, Lily and Doss appear to have been herded, if not into hell, then to a place or state of being where they will be more definitely condemned to punishment. David should be the only character exempted from sharing the same fate as Lily, Doss, and Leroy, but he isn't, and when the play is done, we—as an audience, as witnesses to tragedy—should wonder why not. David's innocence is prevalent throughout, especially when it comes to seeking to understand the true nature of his place within society. He demonstrates a willingness for purity even though he is surrounded by people who are attempting to regain theirs. His performance battles with the divide between these two versions of the world, and this confusion and earnestness manifests most prominently in the final act, which, although it adds to the tension, is still drowned out by the fear plaguing Lily and Doss. Unfortunately, David at the end is led by the figure to the river, and while this might not be fair, whether one is interpreting this from a doctrinal or colloquial sense, we must be reminded Wright's work isn't concerned with fairness; it is concerned with the telling of what should be told, of presenting situations, people, and concepts that prompt further questions that unveil a deeper understanding of the world. *The Delights of Memory* is a testament to Wright's grappling with the complexities of selfishness, with the consequences that result even from inaction, and with accepting that we alone, regardless of influence or desire, will determine our ultimate fate.

DISAPPEARANCE, DISAPPEARING, DISAPPEARED

Sebastián Calderón Bentin

TO ENTER THE SPACE of Jay Wright's work is to enter a non-space, or more precisely a pluri-space. In *The Disappearance of Mexico*, the words "disappearance" and "Mexico" begin a dance that moves between slipping and belonging, presence and disappearance, holding us in a space that only theater can create. Words and geography become threads in a ritual process that weaves poetry into place. Near a stream in the middle of the countryside, huddled around a family of Yoruba drums a traveler arrives announcing some "astonishing news" to his old associate:

GAFO: Mexico has disappeared.

NONO: Yo' mama.

GAFO: Truth in virtue of meaning. We are here. And Mexico no longer exists.[1]

Is this just a story, "lies," as Nono later asserts? Or is this "serious business" about "real death," as his old friend Gafo insists? Has Mexico *really* disappeared? The truth, Gafo notes, is "in virtue of meaning." That phrase, "truth in virtue of meaning," has a long history in analytic philosophy, it posits that some sentences can be true because of

1 Wright, *Selected Plays*, vol. 2, 379.

their inherent meaning rather than any fact or referent outside itself.[2] Gertrude Stein's oft-quoted line "a rose is a rose is a rose" stands as one possible variation of this possibility given how serial self-identification (rose = rose = rose) merges meaning and truth within the sentence itself.[3] Gafo's recourse to "truth in virtue of meaning," a phrase repeated later by Dusel, suggests that Mexico's disappearance might not reside with any verifiable fact or concrete historical event but with the landscape of meaning generated by the play itself. Territory is thus not just spatial but temporal, it is dramatic poetry as event, as ritual performance, that allows for multiple landscapes to manifest themselves: Chicago, Banderilla, Barra de Navidad, Zapopan, Jalisco, Zacatecas, Santa Fe, Los Angeles, and many more. Within this semantic geography, truth and meaning cannot be disentangled from each other or from the ritual space enveloping Nono and his visitors, "those of us gathered in this darkness here."

It is in this darkness that disappearance becomes a precondition for presence since Mexico, once announced to have disappeared, reappears like a mind palace of localized memories: "a Sunday in Xico," "the insult from La Pérgola," "that time in Banderilla," and all those "afternoons in the Alameda." Listening to the characters' stories we jump from Matamoros to Xico, from Ajijic to Tlaquepaque, from San Juan de Letrán to Guadalajara, images of Mexican towns, streets and venues pour onto the playing space "the way cities surfaced and faded like smoke." Mexico continually comes to life even though it has "disappeared," the smell of *chipichipi* ("rain drizzle") and *ranchera* music echoing in the air. As the characters reminisce we wonder if this is a bout of nostalgia, an elegy following Mexico's "disappearance," or "the slipperiness of it"? Unfazed, Nono explains, "we can proceed in this ambiguity."

2 Paul Boghossian, "Truth in Virtue of Meaning," *Australasian Journal of Philosophy* 89:2 (2011): 370–374; Célia Teixeira, "Metaphysical analyticity," *Disputatio* 4 (2012): 869–888.

3 Gertrude Stein, *Lectures in America* (London: Virago, 1988), 231.

This ambiguity is revealed to be more personal, part of a longer history between Nono and Gafo, who "really are family," as Dusel observes. It reaches all the way to when they were part of those "*peones, campesinos, ladrones*"[4] in Xalapa. This was until Nono "packed up in a huff, and left" Mexico, breaking "the contract." Now he's been tracked down, first by Gafo, then by Dusel and his two associates, Dieb and Falz. The arrival of these last three having interrupted Gafo's plan:

> You people, you came and got in the way. You see, I had prepared Nono for devastation, something that would give him the strength I see slipping away from him. So I ran down to the water, I bathed my face in it, I said a little prayer. I wanted him to sit here alone for a while, not with memories, some old stories we can't tell anymore.[5]

For all the reminiscences about Mexico, it is not nostalgia that Gafo wants, but for Nono to regain his strength. "You don't seem to be doing so good, Nono," Gafo warns, "the words are as clear as bells, but you don't know what language they're speaking." Gafo's "astonishing news" regarding Mexico's disappearance is revealed to be an act of caring, a devastating challenge with which to awaken Nono out of his disempowering isolation. But Nono, keeper of his own truths, quickly dispels Gafo's melodrama, "the man's a liar. He came to me as death's secretary. He brought me chocolates, and encouraged my tears." Nono's strength, it seems, has never waned, the power of his music and his "care for dead things" have transformed him into something of an anchorite. "You know it's almost like coming upon a monastery out here," Dussel observes, before admitting later, "we heard that you were spiritual."

It is the journey to Nono that makes pilgrims out of Dusel, Dieb, and Falz, the three having formed a "covenant" as part of their sojourn. During their visit, Dieb and Falz present various artefacts, including "a cornucopia of brilliant cloth," to their unwitting host who is left wondering "how to bear witness to these gifts." But the objects are

4 "Peons, peasants, thieves."
5 Wright, *Selected Plays*, vol. 2, 393.

never gifted, they are merely displayed, cluing us to how their bearers are, as Nono points out, "pilgrims who refuse the pilgrimage." This is "the slipperiness of it," agency as refusal, appearance as disappearance, location as oscillation. As Dusel acknowledges, the three of them knew "this wouldn't be an easy passage," but their journey still drove them to Nono, to put him "through that peculiar test of belonging."

As Dusel tests Nono, "there's nothing on you that says you belong here," we wonder how belonging can be measured if countries continuously disappear? How can we belong anywhere if, as Dusel exclaims, *nadie tiene casa en la tierra* ("no one has a home on this earth")? Were the shared reminiscences of Mexico, which "surfaced and faded like smoke," part of the test of belonging? Are elegies and nostalgia the way we belong to a place? The Portuguese have a word for such a condition, *saudade*, from the Latin plural *solitates*, "solitudes." Duarte Nunes de Leão defined it succinctly in the 17th century as the "memory of a thing with the desire for this same thing."[6] Unlike the saccharine glow of certain nostalgic formations, *saudade* is "endowed with a structural ambiguity" which locates it:

> At the intersection of two affections that present absence: the memory of a cherished past that is no more and the desire for this happiness, which is lacking. Pleasure and anxiety: the result is a displaced, melancholic state that aspires to move beyond the finitude of the moment and the errancy of distance.[7]

As an admixture of mourning and gratitude whereby, as Silvio Lima explains, "the present inhales the past, and, in futurition, exhales it," *saudade* expresses a metaphysical condition that understands the impossibility of belonging as tied to our experience with "temporality, finitude, and the infinite."[8] *Saudade* can vibrate with a land and its people as well as a beloved, whose proximity upon our return produces

6 Fernando Santoro, "Saudade," in *Dictionary of Untranslatables*, ed. Barbara Cassin et al. (Princeton, NJ: Princeton University Press, 2014).

7 Santoro, "Saudade."

8 Santoro, "Saudade."

in us that "mix of anxiety and happiness that precedes the moment of arrival."[9] Amid his travels and travails, Nono seems to have developed a place for placelessness, a mastery over *saudade*, or rather, as Michael Taussig suggests, a mastery of non-mastery.[10] It is the wisdom of this non-mastery that the rest of the vagabonds seek. As Dusel confronts Nono, "you seem to have thrown away quite a lot. For a man who spent so much time becoming familiar with places," to which Nono, using an ancient Greek aphorism, replies: *panta rei* ("all things are flowing").[11]

Panta rei and *saudade* become two sides of the same coin. It is precisely because "all things are flowing" that the present can inhale the past, and, in futurition, exhale it—without time there is no memory, without memory there is no flow. It is Nono's embrace of this Heraclitean perspective that produces a particular kind of wisdom. As he reveals to his guests, "I have a genius for dislocating us. I know about Dieb. I sensed Falz. I even reserved a special place for you, Dusel. These are charities incumbent upon the pilgrim."[12] Tracked and sought, Nono seems always one step ahead (or behind), always oscillating, his visitors unable to pin him down. "This landscape is lost on you," Nono warns them.

In this sense Nono is like the bird in Nicandro Castillo's *ranchera*, *La Calandria*, which he sings once the tequila starts flowing:

> *Yo soy como la calandria*
> *Que para formar su nido*
> *Siempre busca rama fuerte*
> *Para no verlo caído.*

> I am like the chalk-browed mockingbird.
> That to form its nest

9 Santoro, "Saudade."

10 Michael Taussig, *Mastery of Non-Mastery in the Age of Meltdown* (Chicago: University of Chicago Press, 2020).

11 Barry Sandywell, *Dictionary of Visual Discourse: A Dialectical Lexicon of Terms* (Farnham, UK: Ashgate, 2011), s.v. "Heraclitean Flux."

12 Wright, *Selected Plays*, vol. 2, 398.

Looks for a strong branch
Not to see it fall.

It is not a home but a nest (*un nido*) that Nono has created in this "peasant atmosphere," a nest of sound and wood, each Batá drum a branch (*una rama*). While home speaks of belonging, nesting is seasonal and transitory. A bird can't belong to their nest the same way a person can't belong to a country since nests, like countries, appear and disappear, moving from place to place: *panta rei*. Nesting and flowing supersede belonging, "a horrible word," Gafo notes. This is the pluri-space *The Disappearance of Mexico* creates, a geographical metaphysics that pulls all characters toward Nono even while accusing him of having no place: "You've never had a place. You are not wanted. You have nothing to want." But these accusations flow right through Nono, "why, thank you, Falz. You've given me everything by taking it all away." We are all, as Nono observes, "souls without a passport." Which is not to deny that places mark us, "you love Mexico," Dusel tells Nono, "and there's a scar where the heart was." In the flow of time, the scars left by these nests are expressions of *saudade*. Lingering scars that prompt Nono to think of himself as an "archaeologist," constantly digging up the past. And yet, what is this ground that requires digging? "A graveyard?" asks Dusel. "Yes, it is a graveyard," Gafo answers, "it is a perfect evening to come home." Home as burial ground marks the flow and finitude of life, the only form of belonging we are truly ever afforded.

Embracing this archaeology, Nono admits, "I have a care for dead things." And how not to think of the dead when "Mexico" and "disappearance" come together? Women in Juarez, the students from Ayotzinapa, local journalists, environmental activists, and many more disappeared and forgotten by the state. "*Cada día, un día de los muertos*," Nono reminds us.[13] In Mexico there are 109,171 persons currently reported missing, 97% of which began disappearing after 2006, the same period when the administration of Felipe Calderón decided to militarize the state's public security apparatus as part of a new phase in the

13 "Every day, a day of the dead."

US-led "war on drugs."[14] During Calderón's presidency the number of murders in Mexico almost doubled, from his first year in 2007 (10,253 nationwide) to 2012 (22,480).[15] As Nono declares while beating the drum: "Dead things! Dead things! The Distrito Federal! Capital of consciousness!" This is the necropolitics of disappearance that the "war on drugs" has catalyzed, not the disappearance of Mexico but the disappearance of *a* Mexico, the dissolution of a nation into a graveyard, one among many other *death-worlds*, to use Achille Mbembe's term, those "new and unique forms of social existence in which vast populations are subjected to living conditions that confer upon them the status of the *living dead*."[16] But is that not what "the nation" has always been? A graveyard? "Yes, it is a graveyard," Gafo reminds us, "it is a perfect evening to come home."

And as Mexico disappears in this way, don't other countries? The execution of protesters in Iran, mass shootings in the United States, sectarian lynching in the Central African Republic, extrajudicial killings in the Philippines, nation after nation disappearing into death-worlds, fueling disorientation, mourning, and waves of revanchist nostalgia. Each disappearance revealing the precarious promise of the nation-state, a fiction which seems less and less able to cover the stink of the corpses that sustain it.

These disappearances requires vigorous ritual activity with which to process so much grief, accelerating lamentations, as Dusel notes, "these village ceremonials and funerals don't ask for witnesses." As

14 EFE, "'El peligro es mucho, es continuo': México cierra el 2022 con 109,000 desaparecidos," *Telemundo 52*, December 27, 2022, http://www .telemundo52.com/noticias/mexico/mexico-cierra-2022-con-mas-de-cien -mil-desaparecidos/2358661/; "México: Ante los más de 100.000 desaparecidos, la ONU insta al gobierno a combatir la impunidad," *Noticias ONU*, May 17, 2022, https://news.un.org/es/story/2022/05/1508892.

15 Patrick Corcoran, "What to Keep, What to Throw Away from Calderon Presidency," *InSight Crime*, Nov. 30, 2012, https://insightcrime.org/news/ analysis/what-to-keep-what-to-throw-away-from-calderon-presidency.

16 Achille Mbembe, *Necropolitics* (Durham, NC: Duke U. Press, 2019), 92.

bodies disappear, there is no time for witnesses, and often there is no witnessing to be had. But these disappearances also challenge us to think beyond the nation, that is, beyond *belonging*, that horrible word. This is where Wright opens a path for us, beyond necropolitics, where we recognize each other first and foremost as "souls without a passport." It is from here that new covenants might arise, not with the nation but with each other, vagabonds instead of nationals, a new form of peripatetic subjectivity that shares the scars of *saudade* while embracing the flow of impermanence. *Nadie tiene casa en la tierra*, this really is the slipperiness of it, and as Wright assures us, "we can proceed in this ambiguity."

THE RADICAL PERFORMANCE OF GETTING LOST

Multiplicity in *The Possible Impossibility of Leaving Home*

Daniel Woody

We will never ask what a book means, as signified or signifier; we will not look for anything to understand in it. We will ask what it functions with, in connection with what other things it does or does not transmit intensities, in which other multiplicities of its own are inserted and metamorphosed, and with what bodies without organs it makes its own converge.[1]

ATLANTA, the hit TV show on FX, tells the story of Earn, manager of new rap sensation Paper Boi, as he navigates their newfound fame and entry into the predominantly white music industry. Despite the straightforward premise, the show occasionally departs into mysterious, eerie territory. For example, "Three Slaps,"[2] the debut episode of the third season, starts by depicting two never-before-seen characters: a Black man and a White man who chat as they fish aboard a small boat. The white man tells the visibly uneasy Black man that the souls of dead Black people linger just below the water's surface. Suddenly, dozens of Black arms emerge from the dark water and seize the Black man.

At precisely that moment, a young boy, another new character, wakes, and it becomes clear that these men were merely characters in a

1 Gilles Deleuze and Félix Guattari, *A Thousand Plateaus: Capitalism and Schizophrenia*, trans. Brian Massumi (Minneapolis, MN: University of Minnesota Press, 1987), 4.

2 *Atlanta*, season 3, episode 1, "Three Slaps," directed by Hiro Murai, written by Stephen Glover and Donald Glover, aired Mar 24, 2022, on FX.

nightmare. We watch this young boy struggle in school and with his strict family before Child Protective Services moves him into a foster home. The foster family appears to be kind, but behind closed doors, they rename the boy, nearly starve him, and force him to work long hours of domestic labor. The boy, able to read the signs, makes a narrow escape before the family attempts a group suicide, driving the car off a cliff and into a river. The boy returns home, wiser for the wear, with a new respect for his struggling family—clearly, he will be able to succeed in school and life. The episode ends when our protagonist Earn wakes up; it had all been a dream.

This special episode demonstrates the power of the Black imagination, the power of escaping into other realms, into the deepest recesses of our unconsciousness to tap into a collective truth. The imaginary space is itself a type of expressive, performative utterance in which the unconscious is the subject/actor and the conscious is the object/audience. In other words, the dream allows the change (physical, psychological, or spiritual) to occur in the dreamer's life.

This spiritual, performative work dominates Jay Wright's oeuvre, particularly in *The Possible Impossibility of Leaving Home*. In this multilingual, elliptical play, Wright creates a neutral space for characters (and readers) to reimagine themselves. These characters appear to both know each other, and not, they rediscover repressed memories, or perhaps they, at last, put them to rest, and all of this occurs in an unspecified, perhaps real, perhaps conjured space. In this space, boundaries of time, geography, obligation, and even morality fade away, and there is reason to believe that if these characters can interpret the signs and symbols on their journey, they will arrive altered and improved; they might finally be able to wake up or rest in peace.

More specifically, Wright reconfigures our preconceived notions of geographical space by performing a broad pastiche of world mythologies, simultaneously embracing and critiquing, shifting in and out of various performances of identity, ultimately making a statement about the literary act itself: to read is to perceive multiplicities in all things.

The Possible Impossibility of Leaving Home opens with the protagonist, Filo, admiring an orchid in an undisclosed location in the mountains. A local boy joins him, and Filo explains that he is familiar with the region but has lost his way. Then, Filo meets a few other lost travelers: a poet/composer named Bron and "Three Pilgrims" looking for the nearby river. They discuss art, time, and music; they drink, sing, and dance together; and a mysterious woman and young girl occasionally appear, silent, lingering in the background.

Filo's conversations with Bron and the local boy are particularly dialectical; they interrogate one another perhaps to move closer to or realize some unspecified truth: perhaps concrete details about where they are, how they got there, the power of the orchid, etc. But, also, more abstract information: what traumas have they experienced or witnessed, and how should they proceed in their lives? However, Filo constantly evades even the very act of questioning; his relationship with the boy is often openly hostile: the boy scolds him for his language, evasion in conversation, and stealing the orchid.

The boy complains that the group's behavior disrespects the "sacred ground" they occupy. Still, he supports the group by bringing wine from the village, giving Filo the orchid (though somewhat crushed), and revealing that the mysterious woman is his mother. Filo gifts the boy his ruana, and in return, the boy agrees to save his place in this land. The play ends with the group going off together towards the river, singing, while the woman and her children remain, feasting on the party's leftovers.

Although whatever transaction or contract the exchange of the orchid and ruana symbolizes remains hidden, it sets the characters on a path toward resolution, or at least an attempt at one. This narrative structure, overall, zeroes in on the moments in slave narratives that detail the spiritually transformational power of systems of escape.

For example, in her 1861 book, *Incidents in the Life of a Slave Girl*, Harriet Jacobs, under the pseudonym Linda Brent, details the significant events of her life, subverting sentimental norms by ending her novel not in marriage but freedom. She describes her method of escaping slavery: living seven years in a 9′ × 7′ garret, only three feet tall at its highest point, so that her captor would exhaust his efforts in locating her. Katherine McKittrick points out:

> The garret can be conceptualized as usable paradoxical space, which opens up a different way to observe slavery and underscores the geographic shape of mystery. That is, Brent [Jacobs] is a black woman who is positioned across (rather than inside or outside, or inevitably bound to) slavery while in the garret. The garret locates her in and amongst the irrational workings of slavery as a witness, participant, and fugitive. These multiple subject positions [...] gesture to several different geographic possibilities and experiences, such as places seen, remembered, hoped for, and avoided by Brent [Jacobs].[3]

In other words, Jacobs occupied a liminal, geographic space in which she would move from being enslaved to free, a space fertile for her mind, both for its memory and imagination. "Paradoxical" in that, although trapped in an area not much larger than a coffin, that same space awakens her ability to visualize and realize her freedom. Indeed, Jacobs escapes to the North, where she can eventually become a leader in the abolitionist movement and tell this story.

The setting of Wright's play operates as a "paradoxical, usable space" in a similar fashion. Although the characters do not seem to fully understand where they are, why they are there, or how they will continue their journeys, they connect to a more profound sense of themselves and make significant spiritual progress. Further, the elliptical nature of the play allows the reader to include themself in meaning-making, freeing them from any authorial agenda.

Though it pales in comparison to the stakes in both Wright's play and Jacobs's narrative, an example of my own experience navigating this "geographic space of mystery" might be particularly illustrative. In late

3 Katherine McKittrick, "The Last Place They Thought Of: Black Women's Geographies," in *Demonic Grounds: Black Women and the Cartographies of Struggle* (Minneapolis: University of Minnesota Press, 2006), 42–43.

2014, as a graduate student in a creative writing program in Chicago, I felt trapped: trapped, of course, by the heaping amounts of debt I was inviting into my life, trapped by the idea that my intellectual, romantic, and spiritual endeavors would amount to nothing more than a collection of failures, and trapped by a sudden inability to write in a voice that felt like my own, a voice with authenticity and consequence. I could not find a form for what I perceived in the depths of my soul: intangible, inarticulable grief. What's more, I started this program just after Michael Brown's death at the hands of the police and, a few months later, the police's use of excessive force that resulted in an immediate family member's hospitalization.

Not too long before this, shortly after George Zimmerman murdered Trayvon Martin, a police officer pulled me over—I had been speeding. He forced me to stand out on the highway, pointing at me, saying, "I'm not sure what else you have done, but I *am* sure that you are a criminal." My hands were trembling so much that I shoved them into my pockets. His hands went immediately to his gun: "Slowly take your hands out of your pockets," he commanded in a calm, quiet voice. I knew that a wrong move could have resulted in my death.

What a time to start a graduate program! I knew that I was interested in conceptual art and writing, but the community was lousy with scandals; for example, one artist used Michael Brown's autopsy as the content for a performance, highlighting the description of Brown's penis for more effect. And another tweeted in the voice of Mammy from *Gone with the Wind*. A third, the editor of a leading journal, home to conceptual and avant-garde writing, projected racist language behind her during a poetry reading to make her performance more provocative.

How could I make art when the venues and the community seemed utterly problematic? How could I make art when I felt so insecure about my physical safety? How could I write if I could not even find the words to speak about these incidents to my teachers, classmates, friends, family, and even myself?

So, the following year, I began to walk, simply walk, long journeys from my home on the West Side of Chicago to the Loop, a distance of about five miles that would take me over two hours. These walks were efficient; I needed to make it to my lectures on time, so I was careful not to get lost. As I continued, I would leave earlier and earlier, meandering, taking a new route each time. I'm not sure if I really noticed the city or the environment for the first month, but soon it was all I could see. I noticed that I had a habit of avoiding stepping on fallen leaves. It was a sort of unconscious game: "leaf" no trace.

One leaf in particular, though, brought more into my consciousness. The leaf was striking. It was still somewhat green—it had fallen too early—and tiny circular indentations covered its surface. It occurred to me that I saw this leaf as a metaphor for the black body riddled with gunshot wounds. In an attempt to circumvent my grief, I had found myself there, facing it quite directly. For the next six months, when I walked, I would take pictures of single leaves wherever I saw them, sometimes stopping to test my thoughts on what they were saying.

I rejoiced in these leaves. I sculpted them, photographed them, painted them, wrote poems about them, engraved them, cried over them, and shared them with anyone who would make the time.

In other words, my grief led to the practice of searching, which led to the recognition of the symbols, which ultimately culminated in meaning-making: a visual poem and installation that captured how I felt at the moment and allowed me to move on, at least emotionally. And what's more, I had created a liminal space, a performative space, a laboratory that allowed me to detach from my various performances—as a Black man, a graduate student, a poet, a person who must, as Prufrock laments, "prepare a face to meet the faces" and who must still do the dishes and work extra jobs—inhabiting a space to imagine and build a new self, a space to gaze critically at these other selves, a fertile, sacred space for my spirit to heal and flourish.

It is no doubt that any reader of Wright's work would be able to remember or create this kind of performative reflection concerning their own spiritual trials. There is space, for example, for my experience with the leaves on the same stage as Bron's experience with the orchid. In other words, this "paradoxical usable space" of the play can be exploited by each actor during performances of the play. Since each character is a lost traveler, then there is space for each actor to interrogate their own realities, to perform rituals that are ancillary to the text, to devise sibling journeys, perhaps in rehearsal to deepen their embodiment of the role, or perhaps devised physical enactments of the tension between attachment and ascension.

MAPPING THE PLAY

Although the trajectory of *The Possible Impossibility of Leaving Home* is quite direct—a single setting with a limited number of characters—the number of references and allusions is quite substantial. A closer look at the puzzling, contradictory geographical references, in particular, leads to a more complex and conflated web of world mythologies.

Let's start with Filo's sense of where he is at the start of the play. He tells the boy that he is on his way to "a little bit past Phillipsburg, on route 135." There are many possible real-world locations for both Phillipsburg and Route 135, but none where they intersect. Perhaps this is a moment where he has trouble with his memory, is confused, or perhaps it is a red herring; the road outside Philipsburg, Quebec is Route 133, which connects Phillipsburg to other places Bron mentions: Pike River, Henryville, and Iberville. Bron even teases Filo for acting like "the governor of the province."[4] However, the landscape bears a striking resemblance to Jay Wright's vicinity not too far from the Canadian border in Bradford, Vermont. There, Route 135 follows along the Connecticut River.

This geographical conflation sets the tone for many other overlapping boundaries of identity and geography. And yet, despite these references likely pointing to Vermont/Quebec, the local boy with whom Filo converses speaks Spanish as his native language.[5] It is as if these characters inhabit multiple geographic spaces simultaneously.

4 Wright, *Selected Plays*, vol. 2, 421.
5 When Filo tries to charm the boy, Filo uses Spanish, and in several moments when the boy is frustrated, angry, or passionate he switches to the Spanish language.

More striking geographical references puncture the surface as Bron and Filo continue talking. They discuss their time driving in and near Wildflecken, a tiny village in the Rhön Mountains of Germany. It was an essential site during WW II, the site of a displaced persons camp holding Russian, French, and Belgian POWs and a critical US victory late in the war. The region was nicknamed "top of the rock" and thought a hardship post continuing into the Cold War, as unpredictable weather made it easy to die of exposure.

On this drive through the mountains, they discover a "body" that appears to have come out of the darkness. Filo describes it as "A body that gave you an opportunity to touch something deep within yourself." Bron clarifies: "There was a ceremony, then?" "We never stopped," Filo answers.[6] The conversation ends before we can grasp what exactly they mean. Perhaps they conjured the sacred space of the play to finally confront a traumatic sight of a dead soldier they had repressed. Given Jay Wright's military experience stationed in Germany, it's no leap of the imagination to consider this location steeped with memories of loss, grief, and a desire to escape.[7] So, perhaps this is the site of the character's initial wound. Alternatively, maybe the "body" was, in fact, a body of water with the power to transport them to a new reality.

Although the play moves along quickly, leaving this moment unexplained, there is room here for directorial elaboration. What kind of ritual could transport the travelers to this place? Or, what performance, be it physical, musical, or poetic, could mark the transition from the fragmented memory to the setting of the mountains? Perhaps the actors might themselves interrogate the grammar of trauma to extend and exploit this moment.

The next geographical reference is even less explicit. Bron mentions to the silent woman that he "didn't set foot on this land until [he] had

---

6 Wright, *Selected Plays*, vol. 2, 425.

7 On Wright's military service, see William L. Andrews, et al., eds., *Concise Oxford Companion to African American Literature* (Oxford: Oxford Univ. Press, 2001), 446.

permission."[8] The boy pleads with Filo to "abide by the rules" because he is on "sacred ground." The boy's spoken Spanish, coupled with the spirituality of the space, leads me to consider that possible locales include not only the Appalachian Mountains of Southeastern Quebec and the Rhön Mountains of Germany but also indigenous land somewhere in Latin America.

The arrival of the three pilgrims confirms this; they seek the Barba de Chivo River, a river that both Filo and I cannot seem to locate on any map of the living world.[9] In Spanish, *barba* is literally "beard" while *chivo* is "kid" as in "young goat," or colloquially, "young boy." So, the phrase could be translated as "Goatee" or even as "Goatsbeard," a kind of poisonous flower that grows on moist ridges near streams. Or perhaps these men are looking for a river nicknamed after where this flower grows. Or maybe they are looking for someone nicknamed Barba de Chivo who presides over this river domain. The reader does not have access to the specifics of their journey, which leaves room for performances of the play to make these decisions based on other criteria, perhaps the actors' identities.

The boy brings the group some wine, and the pilgrim mentions that, of course, the river spirits would never "leave [them] dry," implying that the boy, the woman, and her daughter are river spirits.[10] Filo describes a journey around Guadalajara: Tepic, Magdalena, Tequila, and Tapatía.[11] He sings a song about Guadalajara. As they talk, Bron makes even more geographical references, the Niger and the Ogun, the two major rivers of West Africa. The characters appear to be from everywhere and nowhere.

The ambiguity and conflation of these geographical references create a unique opportunity for set design. The number of geographical references indicates that the exact location isn't important. So, set

8 *Selected Plays*, vol. 2, 426.

9 *Selected Plays*, vol. 2, 431.

10 *Selected Plays*, vol. 2, 434.

11 *Selected Plays*, vol. 2, 437–438.

designers should feel free to append or alter these references to suit the identities of their performers and their own lived experiences.

COMPARATIVE MYTHOLOGIES

Flowing through many of these geographical references are, of course, rivers and references to river spirits. What to make of this emphasis on the river? Like much of Jay Wright's work,[12] this sent me on a quest to understand possible allegorical interpretations. Graf and Johnston put it best:

> Rivers that must be crossed are in fact one of the most common features of Underworld geographies; by at least the classical period, popular Greek belief developed the idea that coins buried with the dead would ensure that Charon, the infernal ferryman, would transport the soul into the Underworld.[13]

The more we get to know this landscape, the more it feels like a depiction of the underworld's rivers: the Styx, the Acheron, and the Lethe. The river Styx, also known as the River of Hatred, demarcates the borders of the underworld in Dante's depiction:

> And as we sailed the course of this dead channel,
>   before me there rose up a slimy shape that said:
> "Who are you, who come before your time
>   And I spoke back, "Though I come, I do not stay;
>   but who are you, in all your ugliness
> "You see that I am one who weeps," he answered.

12 According to the biography at the Poetry Foundation, "Weaving together various world mythologies and cultures, Wright's poetry reflects the influence of his birthplace in the American Southwest, as well as the heritage of his African ancestry. His poems explore history from this multicultural standpoint and often take the form of allegorical journeys and spiritual quests" ("Jay Wright," Poetry Foundation, 2010, https://www.poetryfoundation.org /poets/jay-wright).

13 Fritz Graf and Sarah Iles Johnston, *Ritual Texts for the Afterlife: Orpheus and the Bacchic Gold Tablets* (New York: Routledge, 2007), 97.

And then I said to him: "May you weep and wail
  stuck here in this place forever, you damned soul,
   for, filthy as you are, I recognize you."
  With that he stretched both hands out toward the boat
  but, on his guard, my teacher pushed him back:
 "Away, get down there with the other curs!"
  And then he put his arms around my neck
  and kissed my face and said, "Indignant soul,
  blessed is she in whose womb you were conceived.
  In the world this man was filled with arrogance,
  and nothing good about him decks his memory;
  for this, his shade is filled with fury here.[14]

Here, Dante greets a dead spirit with curiosity, suspicion, and animosity,
much like Filo treats nearly every other character. The characterization
"you, who come before your time" resonates with the characterization
of Bron, a man "out of his time." Or, perhaps Bron refers to Phlegyas,
who ferries Dante across the river, condemned there for setting fire to
Apollo's temple at Delphi. Bron, too, seems preoccupied with a faint
traumatic memory of a temple.

In Greek mythology, however, it is the river Acheron which leads
into Hell, and Charon who does the ferrying.[15] Charon must be paid
for his services in the form of an *obol*, sometimes described as a coin,
as a ritual, or as actual food or sustenance for the journey.[16] Bron and
Filo discuss such a ritual during their time in the mountains of Germany,
and Filo asks Bron for "sustenance."

14 Dante Alighieri, *Dante's Inferno: The Indiana Critical Edition*, trans. and
ed. Mark Musa (Bloomington: Indiana University Press, 1995), 8.31–48.
15 According to the Theoi Project's online encyclopedia of Greek my-
thology, https://www.theoi.com/greek-mythology/encyclopedia-c.html.
16 See Susan T. Stevens, "Charon's *Obol* and Other Coins in Ancient Fu-
nerary Practice," *Phoenix* 45.3 (Autumn 1991): 215–229. In her essay, Stevens
describes how the word *obol* becomes conflated with the word *viaticum*
(eucharist or holy communion) in Catholic traditions.

Along these same lines, these characters could also be seeking the river Lethe, also known as the River of Forgetfulness. According to Plato, good souls acquire the knowledge of what constitutes a good life through philosophy, and, in the journey of the afterlife, they have an opportunity to choose the nature of their reincarnation. Graf and Johnston write:

> Whereas some souls choose their new incarnations hastily and badly, distracted by the glittering riches associated with particular lives, those who have learned restraint and who possess knowledge make a more careful choice and enter upon a new life that will be relatively virtuous and free of pain. The challenges are not over yet, however: having chosen their next lives, the souls journey across the scorching Plain of Oblivion and eventually reach the River of Forgetfulness. All of the souls drink from this river, but "those who were not saved by their good sense (*phronēsis*) drank more than they needed to and forgot everything [that they had learned]." These souls begin their new life at square zero, no further ahead than they were when they began the previous one. The good-plus, in contrast, drink in moderation and carry some of what they have learned into the next incarnation.[17]

In other words, the Plain of Oblivion is another one of these "paradoxical spaces" in which souls prepare to drink from the river and continue into their next life. With this in mind, the scenes that describe Filo, Bron, and the three pilgrims drinking wine fetched by the river spirits could suggest a more potent elixir. Or, perhaps these characters have already had their fair share from the Lethe, which would explain their fragmented memories.

While these echoes of Greek rivers are undoubtedly fascinating, other examples of world myths are worthy of discussion. Jay Wright spent substantial time studying Igbo, Yoruba, and Komo religions, which led me to research whether the temple "Orita" that Bron mentions might relate to Nigerian culture. Mary Helen Specht provides a valuable introduction:

17 Graf and Johnson, *Ritual Texts*, 102.

In the traditional culture of southwestern Nigeria, if you're looking for ghosts or spirits or even Death, the "Orita Meta," a place where three or more paths meet, will accommodate. The Yoruba believe that crossroads are liminal spaces, thresholds where humans and ancestors, the living and the dead, exist on a cusp. Even in the modern hustle-bustle of West Africa, crossroads are still places you're likely to find shrines and offerings to the spirits.[18]

With this in mind, the familiarity and strangeness of each character and symbol make much more sense. Geographically, the play is set in an area where a road, a river, and a path to a village all meet, a "liminal space" where people come and go, and spiritually, a place where characters seem to be either living, the souls of the dead, or spiritual entities. When Bron speaks of a ritual and a shrine at Orita, perhaps he is actually describing his journey to the "sacred grounds." Specht continues with a discussion of the *abiku*:

> [*Abiku* is] the Yoruba word for spirit-child or a child caught in an unending cycle of birth and death with the same human mother, unable to choose between the world of the spirits and that of his human family. *Abikus* come from a spirit world inhabited by beautiful yet sinister beings, and in order for human parents to prevent the abiku child from returning to the spirit world, they have to find hidden charms that link the child to his or her spirit companions.[19]

This concept of *abiku* resembles the boy and his obsession with protecting the orchid: it ties his soul to the land, and Filo's theft could condemn the boy to the spirit world. When Filo offers his ruana, a regional item of clothing that perhaps tethers Filo to the human world, he has saved the boy from this plight. Or, perhaps Filo truly is the boy's father, on a quest to find a way to bring his son back home from the underworld. Specht elaborates:

18 Mary Helen Specht, "At the Crossroads: In Search of the Nigerian Abiku," *World Literature Today* 87.5 (2013): 34.
19 Specht, 34.

Apparently all *abiku* are by nature sadists in the spirit world. And while a few might become humanists during their time in the human world […] it was usually too late. They had already arranged a time of death with their spirit companions before birth, so unless they could break ties with those companions, their fate was sealed.[20]

The boy has little respect for Filo at the start of the play, but at the end of the play, they exchange gifts and the boy remains behind with his mother and sister as the others continue to the river.

In addition to the connection to the rivers of the Greek underworld and the *abiku* of the Yoruba, there exist countless other possible references: the countless Greek myths of naiads, nymphs, and sirens; the *kappa*, the mischievous child spirits of Japanese folklore; the Rhinemaidens of Wagner's *Ring Cycle* ; etc. But perhaps the most compelling echo of river spirit mythology is Mami Wata.

MAMI WATA

Depictions of Mami Wata proliferate in many African religions and throughout the African diaspora. Henry John Drewal explains that she is a spirit to whom one makes a substantial sacrifice or gift and with whom, in return, one makes a contract to achieve wealth and/or fertility. She is typically depicted as a mother, with her children nearby, or as a hybrid creature, part woman, part fish, but someone exotic, someone who hails from a faraway place. Drewal elaborates:

> [D]epictions of her have been profoundly influenced by representations of ancient, indigenous African water spirits, European mermaids, and snake charmers, Hindu gods and goddesses, and Christian and Muslim saints. […] Her very name is in pidgin English, a language developed to lubricate trade. The countless millions of enslaved Africans who were torn from their homeland and forcibly carried across the Atlantic between the sixteenth and nineteenth centuries as part of this "trade" brought with them their beliefs, practices, and arts honoring Mami

20 Specht, 37.

Wata and other ancestral deities. Reestablished, visualized, and revitalized, in diaspora Mami Wata emerged in new communities and under different guises, among them Lasiren, Yemanja, Santa Marta la Dominadora, and Oxum.[21]

Like the symbol of the river itself, Mami Wata has many flexible, overlapping implications on Wright's play. Perhaps the mysterious, inaccessible woman lingering in the background is in fact an allusion to Mami Wata, and the boy acts as her agent, securing Filo's ruana as a sacrifice.

The idea that the play could reference tales of Mama Wati coupled with the idea that the mysterious setting of the play could be somewhere in Mexico, leads me to suspect that Wright has cleverly incorporated tales of La Llorona, the river spirit who roams lands near rivers where she is rumored to have drowned her children, a tale popular in Jay Wright's hometown of Albuquerque, New Mexico.[22] In effect, he creates a new amalgamation of Mami Wati.

THE ORCHID

Whether we read the boy as an abiku negotiating between the spirit world and the human world, or we read him as the agent of Mami Wata or other river spirits, there remains the question of the orchid. As I mentioned above, the play starts and ends with this central, mysterious object.

In many cultures, people thought orchids could enhance fertility and increase the likelihood of conceiving a male child. For example, in his cultural history of orchids, Jim Endersby notes that Moctezuma, emperor of the Aztecs, regularly drank a special kind of hot chocolate flavored with the extracts of a vanilla orchid, a substance they called

---

21 Henry John Drewal, "Mami Wata: Arts for Water Spirits in Africa and Its Diasporas," *African Arts* 41.2 (Summer 2008): 60–61.
22 Gina Dimuro, "Inside the Legend of La Llorona, the Vengeful Spirit of the Southwest," *All that's Interesting*, Sept. 21, 2022, https://allthatsinteresting.com/la-llorona.

tlilxóchitl (literal translation, "black flower"), at least according to the accounts of Francisco Hernandez, a Spanish botanist who spent substantial time in "New Spain."[23]

The name "orchid" itself is derived from the ancient Greek *orkhis* for "testicle," perhaps labeled by the first known botanist Theophrastus, not because of any source in history or literature, but because he found the shape of the root tubers to have an uncanny resemblance to the testicles.[24]

The origin myth of the orchid flower often goes like this: a man named Orchis was born the child of a satyr and a nymph. During one particular bacchanalia, Orchis attempted to rape a maenad or nymph (depending on the account) but was caught in the act. As punishment, the women ripped his body (or his genitals) to shreds (or summoned beasts to do their bidding) and where the pieces fell grew orchids.[25] However, this account appears nowhere in the Roman or Greek canons.[26]

Endersby's most significant contribution is his discovery of the source of this mythological tale: a French writer by the name of Louis Liger. Liger wrote *Le jardinier fleuriste et historiographe*, a book that purports to document the mythical origins of common flowers but, instead, imagines them. Liger writes:

> 'Twas at the Festival of Bacchus, that Orchis, like others of the same Character, being in Drink, committed the most disorderly Actions that can be imagined. Being the Son of A Rural God, he thought he might do anything with Impunity; and his brutish Passion blinded him so far, that

23 Jim Endersby, "The Name of the Orchid," in *Orchid: A Cultural History* (Chicago: University of Chicago Press, 2016), 58.

24 Sandra Knapp, "Roots of Love," *Extraordinary Orchids* (Chicago: Univ. of Chicago Press, 2021), 41.

25 This can be found in encyclopedias, introductions to scholarly scientific studies on orchids, and on various gardening resources, but was nowhere to be found in encyclopedias and indices of Greek and Roman mythology..

26 Endersby, 60.

he had the Insolence to lay Hands on one of the Priestesses of Bacchus, for which he was punished upon the Spot; for the Priestess did so incense the Bacchantes or Assistants at the Festival against him, that they fell upon him and pulled him almost to pieces; and all that his Father could obtain of the Gods, was to have him turn'd into a Flower, which was to perpetuate his Name, as a lasting Stain upon his Memory.[27]

Endersby notes that this account from Liger conflates several other floral origin stories (e.g., Narcissus, Pentheus, Hyacinth) and Ovid's *Metamorphoses* (where, for example, Daphne escapes Apollo by transforming into a laurel tree). Despite the falseness of Liger's narrative, Endersby concludes that there is no doubt that the orchid would invoke sexual associations. This conclusion makes sense when one examines them purely in terms of their appearance: they are delicate, elegant, and fragile, and as a result, in popular culture, they have often been linked to a sort of sacred, seductive innocence, and at the same time, death.

Jay Wright's orchid, then, also serves as a symbol with layered interpretations. Filo could seek the orchid to return to the living world with some advantage; he mentions to Bron that he would like to be a father. Or, perhaps the boy wishes to protect the orchid as it symbolizes his actual life force. In any case, it is enough for the play's audience to understand that the orchid is significant.

The orchid can play a crucial role in the performances of the play; perhaps the actors ought to develop their own relationship with the meaning of the flower, a relationship kept secret from the other cast members. The actors can explore this relationship physically; how an actor might approach the orchid, carry it, worship it, dance for it, sing to it, etc. The possibilities for interpretation are endless.

CONCLUSION

In their introduction to *A Thousand Plateaus*, Deleuze and Guattari first describe the traditional book: the root-book. In the same way

---

27 Cited in Endersby, 59.

that roots imitate the form of the tree above, the root-book attempts to capture the qualities of real life. This mimicry leads towards a perhaps erroneous, Manichean way of thinking, or as Deleuze puts it: "one leads to two." Jay Wright's play resists this kind of reflection of the world; as we read the play, we must simultaneously carry the notions that the setting, for example, is the underworld, a mountainous region in Mexico, Germany, Canada, or Africa, and a vision/dream. And, we must simultaneously see the characters as figments of Filo's unconscious, other lost souls converging at a common crossroads, and actual people lost in the woods.

This ambiguity connects to Deleuze and Guattari's description of the rhizome, an underground, tubular stem that carries within it all possibilities, i.e., "shelter, supply, movement, evasion, and break-out."[28] In other words, rhizomes, unlike roots, grow and travel in any direction underground, breaching the surface and producing a whole new offshoot of the plant or performing whatever role supports the plant as a whole. "A rhizome may be broken, shattered at a given spot, but it will start up again on one of its old lines, or on new lines," they write.[29] To illustrate the difference between a root system and a rhizome, they write:

> The wasp is nevertheless deterritorialized, becoming a piece in the orchid's reproductive apparatus. But it reterritorializes the orchid by transporting its pollen. Wasp and orchid, as heterogeneous elements, form a rhizome. It could be said that the orchid imitates the wasp, reproducing its image in a signifying fashion (mimesis, mimicry, lure, etc.) [...But] there is neither imitation nor resemblance, only an exploding of two heterogeneous series on the line of flight composed by a common rhizome that can no longer be attributed to or subjugated by anything signifying.[30]

To engage with Wright's play, one must not merely seek an explanation but must actively perform the multiplicity that Wright's play

28 Deleuze and Guattari, *A Thousand Plateaus*, 7.
29 Deleuze and Guattari, 9.
30 Deleuze and Guattari, 10.

exhibits: the reader must simultaneously question each moment and yet resist the act of formal investigation. Or, as Deleuze puts it, the reader must be careful to "make a map, not a tracing."[31] To trace would be to copy a part of a map, ascribing a hierarchical relationship between source and product. Indeed, as demonstrated in this essay, parts of *The Possible Impossibility of Leaving Home* can be traced. But it is only in the layering of these tracings that the multiplicity can be perceived.

31 Deleuze and Guattari, 13.

LEMMA

Jay Wright's Idiorrhythmic American Theater

Will Daddario

Originally published in *Pamiętnik Teatralny* 70, no. 4 (2021): 121–140, https://doi.org/10.36744/pt.985. Many thanks to the editorial team of that journal and to Michal Kobialka for inviting me to contribute.

SPATIAL HISTORY, OR WHERE IS JAY WRIGHT?

THE FIGURE OF JAY WRIGHT presents a compelling paradox. He is one of the most highly decorated and esteemed poets in the United States, on the one hand. On the other, this leading voice of American poetry seems to echo within the penumbra cast by canonical literature, producing a sound in a register that only a few can hear.

This essay resists the question "Who is Jay Wright?" with its interrogative weight tied to matters of stable identity, and chooses instead to begin with a spatial investigation framed by the question, "Where is Jay Wright?"

There are two sides to this question. First, when we acknowledge Wright's astonishing body of work, which has garnered many awards and fellowships, and its contribution to the poetry of the Americas, we wonder why we do not often find him in the various anthologies devoted to African American literature and poetry. Given that his writing includes not only fourteen published books of poetry but also more than fifty dramatic works for the theater, we might also puzzle over Wright's absence in *The Kenning Anthology of Poets Theatre* (2010), a volume that specifically seeks to shine light on neglected, hard-to-classify works for the theater by poets in the twentieth century. In other words, when we seek to build a historiographic dossier for Jay Wright, we look for his presence only to ask, "Where is he?" Or, to rephrase the main question as an answer: Wright is absent from the history of Black theater in the United States.

Here, however, I choose to negate that version of the question as well as the statement formed in the question's declarative mode. This constitutes a negation of the negation, insofar as I mark the perception of Wright's historiographic absence but counter it with a clear yet also oblique answer. Where is Jay Wright? He is somewhere else. His is a present absence. He is off conjuring the unthought. He's making new ground for himself. He's producing territory, a territory formed through a unique rhythm of thought and language.

My approach here is not strictly dialectical, but the deployment of the negation of a negation helps to frame the paradox of the living, historical figure of Jay Wright. He is not anthologized with other thinkers from the Black Arts Movement (BAM), for example, because he left that scene. Historians are right, therefore, to exclude him from that group. Likewise, despite the fact that he is both poet and playwright, his absence in anthologies of poets' theater is acceptable, for Wright's musical dramaturgy and the staggering breadth of his source material make of his theatrical work something as yet to be explored in both mainstream- and fringe- theater environments. Thus, Wright's seeming absence and his identity as the poet not anthologized by canonical publications deserves to be rectified not through an alternative historical narrative that would prove how he was or should have been there all along; rather, his absence transforms into a negative presence, one very much *not* operating within canonical territory. My proposal is to negate the underlying premise that he ought to be remembered as a Black American poet (understood as an individual belonging to the set of people known as members of the Black Arts Movement, for example) in order to visit the world he made, and is currently making, on his travels. This world is America, too, but is dissonant when heard alongside the America of BAM and the Black Power Movement. Where is Wright? He's here, in his theater, making America.

Treating *Lemma* in this essay as a work of dramatic literature rhythmically producing territory leads to my primary historiographic maneuver. Overall, I perform a double procedure. I will demonstrate how Wright's work constitutes a historiographic intervention through his arrangement of texts and the methods he deploys to reveal the entanglement of thought systems typically kept apart by academic disciplines. At the same time, I want to forward my claim that Wright's art of arrangement allows his audience (i.e., us) to reflect upon ways in which individuals make themselves out of others' texts and memories, an act of making that ultimately reveals a tangle of intersubjective selves. These selves are not formed from historical certainties; neither are they themselves static in the present. They exist only through their performance. After Wright, to think "American theater" is to think America as the product of a historiographic operation of arrangement and enaction.

MEETING WRIGHT ON HIS GROUND

Lemma builds on an undeniable ritual framework—though "ritual" here carries a precise meaning. Wright's essay "Desire's Design, Vision's Resonance: Black Poetry's Ritual and Historical Voice" (1987) names "a process of separation, transition and incorporation" in the poetry of Christopher Okigbo placing "the poet on the mystic blade."[1] Such a process, also called "ritual," is found in contemporary Black poetry where it shows itself as a mode of knowing the world marked by the valorization of both human intellectual and emotional capacity, the incorporation of multiple forms of historical knowledge (from myth to science), and the tendency to dig beneath one's historical situation to uncover the profound pain and joy that grows there. Such ritual is prevalent in the poetic tradition of Black Americans, as Wright says; yet it is also present in the Afro-Cuban milieu, in cultural remnants of the Gaelic world, and in the theatrical expression of the ancient Greeks,

1 Jay Wright, "Desire's Design, Vision's Resonance: Black Poetry's Ritual and Historical Voice," *Callaloo* 30 (Winter 1987): 23, https://doi.org/10.2307/2930633.

to name but a few specific sites. Thus, the play's ritual form, that is, the way in which historically transmitted linguistic and gestural codes unite the characters with their ancestors while simultaneously preparing the ground of the present for new growth, is not a strictly religious or spiritual undertaking. It is something marked most dominantly by the precise cut it makes in the here and now. This cut—brought to mind by the phrase "poet on the mystic blade"—severs a ritual's performers from the mundanity of the contemporary moment while also suturing those performers to a trans-historical network of people, places, objects, and beliefs that collaborate in the epistemology of a given culture. This dual cut, emerging as both sever and suture, helps to maintain or restore order to the world, though this act of ordering cannot be understood outside the notion of change and transformation. Order and the disorder of transformation fuse through ritual activity, and the success of this fusion relies greatly upon theater's effervescent quality, the way theater accommodates both scripted realities and performers' improvisations.

Lemma begins to come into focus as a theatrical container into which Wright transmits a grouping of historical knowledges for the purpose of ritual transformation. To this combination of ideas, I want to add a third ingredient, that of polyrhythm. *Lemma*'s undeniable musical sensibility—audible in the opening scene of "voices," the presence of the *agogo* throughout the text, the specific focus on the Lydian mode, etc.—emerges from Wright's polyrhythmic *poieses*. Serendipitously, as I was drafting this essay, I received a package from Wright containing his most recent philosophical examination. The topic of this examination is "rhythm," and the thinking presented in the paper outlines a clear concern of the poet: namely, the need to think rhythm without the notions of time and order. Can we, he wonders, think rhythm as spatial and having shape? His question leads to a mapping of rhythm's edge, that place where states of matter transform into something else, something different from what they have previously been.[2] His philosophical

2 This essay is now included in Jay Wright, *Soul and Substance: A Poet's Examination Papers* (Princeton, NJ: Princeton University Press, 2023).

questions prompt me to think of *Lemma* as taking place on that edge site of transformation, motivated by a polyrhythmic assembly of shapes of thought typically separated from one another within academic discourse, such as Spanish and Gaelic resonances, Western poetry and African epistemologies, and the forms of Ancient Greek theater and Mesoamerican ritual sacrifice.

Wright's rhythm is something that marks him as distinct from Black Arts Movement poets. Where they, acting as what Larry Neal calls the artistic arm of the Black Power Movement, sought to create a vision of a Black national identity that would free African Americans from the oppression of Whiteness and the institutionalized violence of racism, Wright's poetry taps out what might be called the idiorrhythm of Being. This idiorrhythmy rhymes, in part, with what Deleuze calls the univocity of being:

> With univocity, however, it is not the differences which are and must be: it is being which is Difference, in the sense that it is said of difference. Moreover, it is not we who are univocal in a Being which is not; it is we and our individuality which remains equivocal in and for a univocal Being.[3]

Wright's particular rhythmic sensibility and musical dramaturgy, however, in-formed in equal parts by Afro-Cuban jazz, Gaelic myth, Spanish modernism, pre-Socratic philosophy, and other seemingly far-flung reservoirs of cultural expression, sets him apart from Deleuze and asks that we approach his work with an interrogative spirit by continually asking "Where is Wright?," "What is he making?," "How does this all sound?," and "How do we play it?"

Given my particular arrangement of ideas and interpretations up to this point, Wright is hopefully beginning to appear as equal parts poet and historiographer. His plays make a laboratory space, one that should also be called a ritual space, despite the fact that laboratories and rituals are often invoked in completely different settings (or perhaps precisely because of this). That lab-ritual space showcases how

3 Gilles Deleuze, *Difference and Repetition*, trans. Paul Patton (New York: Columbia University Press, 1994), 39.

multiple entangled systems of thought constitute the notion of self. Key to the creation and transformation of self is the notion of rhythm and its ever-unfolding nature. Throughout this paper, I hint at shifts into the sonic register to intimate that historiography comes close to the art of musical production in the way it arranges historical materials and through its belief in the matter of thought. That is, where musicians (including Wright) feel out the texture of frequencies borne within notes they play, historiographers sense the vibration of thought, the degree to which ideas make material changes to society and to the planet. The more historiographers think of their work in relation to music, the more chances exist to play the past in inventive ways that nevertheless remain tethered to historical material. In my case, and with this essay in particular, I am learning from Wright how to play the score of *Lemma* composed by a wildly diverse body of thought and artistic forms.

GETTING ORIENTED: THEMES AND VARIATIONS

As I have written elsewhere,[4] I believe that focusing on the "what-ness" of dramatic literature, which corresponds with "what really happened" in certain schools of historical thought, presumes a single, static thing to be found. I look instead to the arrangement of historical material and listen for harmonies and dissonances produced through the playing of specific arrangements. With this predisposition in mind, I want to share the findings of my field notes, the ideas that arose as I traveled through the map/script/territory that Wright has produced, to help us read the score of his dramatic text. By reading the score, I can sense the possibility of multiple meanings, or at the very least activate the production of meaning so key to thinking since Barthes's declarations in "The Death of the Author" (1967) and subsequent postmodern

4 Will Daddario, "Adorno, Baroque, Gardens, Ruzzante: Rearranging Theatre Historiography," in *Theatre/Performance Historiography: Time, Space, Matter*, eds. Rosemarie K. Bank and Michal Kobialka (New York: Palgrave Macmillan, 2015), 177–197.

variations on that theme. Before sharing those notes and reading that score, let me provide some essential information about the characters, setting, actions, and themes Wright mobilizes in the play.

The opening stage directions diagram the world:

> Lights come up on a sextet of actors, each one carrying a particular property that each will use as a subtle shift in movement in the action that involves that actor—call it a change in direction and a new placement of relationships. The actors move at first in a single line, then begin and carry out a series of differing positions with respect to each other, as though they were looking for the proper and perfect configuration of their group. They choose, and come to a first rest. Each one now sings an individual prologue.[5]

The actors form a sextet. The word "sextet" identifies a group of six, generally, and also, specifically, a musical group of six players. The actors are also musicians, as the instruction "sings an individual prologue" hints. The "singing" is not necessarily the kind of singing one would expect from a soprano or a bass voice; rather, it sounds to me like the singing in which poets across the ages have participated. The "song" is the story and the singing is its telling.

Next, Wright alerts us to objects carried by the actors. Throughout the text, certain objects will receive special attention and, in a sense, come alive. A white cloth carries extreme importance, as though it endows its carrier with a profound responsibility. Similarly, an obsidian knife will, perhaps, bring us into the orbit of Okigbo's poetic ritual incantations. As with the "power objects" (*boli*) of the Bamana and the sacred ritual objects of the Yoruba, these "properties" are endowed with agency and thus actively participate in the arrangement of the ritual action.

As the play progresses, the ritual affixes to a certain temporal window, one that is both past and yet to come (around again). The characters refer to this as the "third hour." "I want to know what happened

5 Wright, *Selected Plays*, vol. 1, 183.

in that third hour,"[6] Bricco says to Fuadach. A few pages later, Lorg tells Bricco, "Fuadach will never tell you what happened in that third hour."[7] Throughout the text, this time signature emerges within the dialogue and then disappears into the background of the action. The third hour has passed, but the characters also work to revive it, as one might recall and relive a memory.

The third hour is most notably a time of the Christian temporal scheme, specifically one of seven dedicated times of prayer. Known as *Terce*, it corresponds, roughly, to 9am, or three hours after dawn. Its original importance is recorded in Acts 2:15 when, during that time, the Holy Spirit descended upon the Apostles. This was precisely fifty days after Easter and gave rise to the holy day known as Pentecost. In *Lemma*, however, this temporal destination, the third hour, a time-space coordinate that some characters can return to via memory but that remains an unseen destination for other characters, is tinted with a distinctly pre- or simply non-Christian color. We see this fact in certain references but also in ways the characters prepare the space with a ritual design on the ground. Altogether, then, the temporal nexus of the third hour evokes something like a neo-Baroque hybrid of Christian (Spanish), Gaelic, West African, Aztec, and other indigenous ritual traditions. The hybridity so common to Baroque and neo-Baroque thinking intentionally destabilizes the ostensible certainty of Christianity's linear and teleological temporal scheme. Here Wright shows his work as a historiographer by making sure that the play's audience understands the specific notions of time and space in which all this action unfolds. This is not *Terce* as woven by Christians. It is more like a *Terce* third space, a liminal threshold of change and transformation that unites physical and spiritual change through one swift passage.

The final sentences of the opening stage direction reveal the importance of arrangement throughout the play. As the characters prepare the space and arrange themselves in different combinations (through dialogue, stage position, etc.), it becomes clear that the group is engaged

6 Wright, *Selected Plays*, vol. 1, 184.
7 *Selected Plays*, vol. 1, 188.

in a kind of ritual invocation. They are attempting to evoke a memory, it seems, or perhaps to distill a pure memory from the overlap of multiple disparate (narratives of) memories. The picture they are seeking to develop involves three sisters, Carmen, Elzbieta, and Peregrinas. At one point, Spalla and Polso, yoked together as a kind of ancient Greek chorus involved in movements of strophe and antistrophe, ask directly "Did the sisters survive?" Ginocchio, another of Lorg's names, replies "No."[8] The specific details of these sisters, their deaths and their engagements with the six main characters who are producing this ritual remembering, becomes the focus of the play's second half. In Wright's opening stage direction, however, at least as much emphasis is placed on the act of arrangement as on the arrangement's actual effect, if not more.

HISTORICO-POETIC ENTANGLEMENT

Playing *Lemma* requires that the spectator discerns the harmonic resonance produced by weaving together multiple systems of thought. One way to do this is to linger on direct citations from existing literary, philosophical, and other historical sources that Wright puts in his characters' mouths. For example, among the prologues sung in the opening moments, Voice D says:

> Her nests, when one comes across them in dreams, lodged in rock-clefts, or the branches of enormous hollow yews, are built of carefully chosen twigs, lined with white horse-hair and the plumage of prophetic birds and littered with the jawbones and entrails of poets.[9]

These words come from Robert Graves's mytho-history *The White Goddess* (1948). In that work, Graves excavated what he believed to be the source of poetry's "true" language; namely, the magical language bound up with the ritual praise of the Moon-Goddess in the Old Stone Age. He claims that the matrilinear origins of this true language were overwritten by the patrilineal heritages of invading/migrating tribes

8 *Selected Plays*, vol. 1, 215.
9 *Selected Plays*, vol. 1, 183, 234.

who sought justification for imposing patriarchal systems of governance. From the 1950s onward, as Fran Brearton argues, much of Graves's poetry attempts to embody precisely the sonic quality of this ancient poetry where "Language itself is a honey trap, words a web in which we can be caught."[10] We could describe the language of *Lemma* in similar terms, and add that Wright subordinates the words' content (i.e., their meaning) to their sonic qualities, which in turn carry the ability to produce magical effects, such as the resurrection of a memory or transportation to the third hour.

There are six of these direct quotations in the play, and the words come from a surprising cadre of historical figures: Robert Graves, Luke the Evangelist, E.M. Forster (from an essay considering the presence of Giorgos Seferis's poetic spirit in C.P. Cavafy's work), the philosopher Elizabeth (G.E.M.) Anscombe, John Donne, and Nicholas of Cusa. Wright's quotations blend together like notes in a chord and produce an invisible yet sensible matrix of thought from which *Lemma*'s action springs.

When we listen to Wright's chord, what do we hear? There is a consideration of poetic genealogy first, or a meditation on how the lives of many poets live within a singular body. Graves, Forster (who comprehends the nested dyad of Seferis and Cavafy), and Donne sing of poetry's ability to enthuse (ἔνθεος, from Ancient Greek) or in-spirit other beings and remind us that poetic language makes palpable the limen between birth and death.

The Graves quotation doubles as a historiographical procedure insofar as it deconstructs the Christian facade erected around earlier religious practices and reinfuses poetry with a magical ability. This is more than a metaphor. Deconstructing actual architectural facades of churches throughout Mexico, for example, would provide access to pre-Christian structures activated within indigenous belief systems. Prayers that took place in those original spaces appear to contemporary Western eyes as arcane magic, and that magic is an analogue to types

10 Fran Brearton, "Robert Graves and The White Goddess," *Proceedings of the British Academy* 131 (2005): 300.

of spirituality practiced by Celtic priests and priestesses for which Forster advocates. Forster's words that "material that has grown old in monasteries and libraries" provide more historiographical intervention, drawing our attention to the distinction between books collected in archives, on the one hand, and the performative capacities of those words, on the other. In the same essay from which Wright's quotation is drawn, Forster likens historical sources motivating Seferis's poetry to a kind of choreography requiring a dancer's body to bring it to life. Cavafy's work, according to Forster, was to sort out where his Greek countryman's poetry failed to attach a body to diagrams of their inherited choreography and to ensure that the historical material's richness did not become but an ornamental source for hollow hymns. Wright is engaged in precisely this activity: a bodying forth of ritual language seeking to ground the sounds of voices in the here and now of the ritual's unfolding. We see this in the way *Lemma* begins with Voices A–F and ends with characters affixed to those voices. Voice D, who speaks Graves's words, lands in the body of Bacán, one of two female characters in the play. The Forster quotation belongs to Polso, the character who generates the ritual diagram on the ground of the performance space and who enters "ringing an *agogo* in a syncopated rhythm."[11]

The last thread in the woven tapestry of poetic genealogy (other than Wright's voice, of course, which pulsates throughout the entire text) ties to John Donne's *Death's Duell* (1632):

> We have a winding sheet in our mothers wombe, which grows with us from our conception, and we come into the world, wound up in that winding sheet, for we come to seek a grave.

Interested in Nancy Selleck's notion of "*material embeddedness* of life and surround," Hester Lees-Jeffries unspools the significance wound up within Donne's reference to sheets. For Lees-Jeffries, such significance ties to an "early-modern textile imaginary" that saw in the common

---

11 Wright, *Selected Plays*, vol. 1, 190. The *agogo* is a bell that comes from Yorubaland and was crucial in religious ceremonies of the Yoruba as well as in *candomblé* ceremonies in the New World.

bedsheet the same material that would eventually become a tool for a midwife's work and at some point, sooner or later, one's own funeral shroud.[12] The sheet therefore links birth, sleep/stillness, and death and signifies this linkage throughout its life as a vibrant object. In *Lemma*, Donne's words come from the mouth of Bricco who, after citing Donne, promptly offers to handle the stage property-actant of the white sheet, which, we have learned by that point, serves a crucial function in the offing of the play's ritual.

Wright accomplishes at least two feats through the poetic family summoned together through his direct quotations. First, he calls our attention to the act of poetizing and the life experiences that tether poetry to bodies, thereby acknowledging poetry's material significance in the world. Words speak of people and things but that speech, when properly arranged, also opens up lines of sight into historical epistemes providing the conditions for poetry's mythic-religio-magical abilities. Perhaps this is where poetry becomes dramatic poetry. Second, the grouping of direct citations not only produces the connection between Graves, Donne, Forster, Seferis, and Cavafy, it also reveals the degree to which those figures were always already connected. This revelation helps us consider the entanglement of knowledge systems that scholars typically keep separated. More specifically, Wright prompts us to wonder how the existing entanglement of these poets' material ideas live on, in, and through his characters' bodies, and perhaps our own, as well.

The web of entangled historical thought also contains strands connecting secular, analytic philosophy, and religious beliefs. Wright illuminates these strands by placing the words of G.E.M. Anscombe in the mouth of Bacán: "thus St. Peter could do what he intended not to do, without changing his mind, and yet do it intentionally."[13] This single

12 Hester Lees-Jeffries, "'Thou Hast Made this Bed Thine Altar': John Donne's Sheets," in *Domestic Devotions in the Early Modern World*, eds. Marco Faini and Alessia Meneghin (Leiden: Brill, 2018), 269–287.
13 Wright, *Selected Plays*, vol. 1, 211.

sentence, which appears at the end of Anscombe's *Intention* (1957), concludes what is otherwise a seemingly areligious, philosophical essay on ethics, action theory, and agency. Wright provides Anscombe with a philosophical partner through the brief passing invocation of the surname Polkinghorne, which the characters in *Lemma* affix to the mysterious Elzbieta (and perhaps, by extension, the sisters Carmen and Peregrina). John Polkinghorne was a British mathematician, physicist, theologian, and Anglican priest whose work consistently invoked the harmonies between science and religion. Thus, taken all together, Wright provides a specific constellation for us to ponder: Elizabeth Anscombe, Elzbieta Polkinghorne, John Polkinghorne.[14] The constellation does not mean something; rather, its identity-as-arrangement produces a container to hold a certain story. In *Lemma*, the words of (female) philosopher Anscombe are spoken by Bacán, one of the play's two female characters, who repeatedly embodies the ghost of Elzbieta, thereby making her memory dance within the play's ritual. The philosophical text that is quoted, when paired with the play's ongoing ritual action, alerts us to the entanglement between theology and science. More than that, Wright alerts his readers that any magic taking place through the play's ritual—i.e., its particular form that both severs and sutures past and/from present, providing order to the transformation of being each character is undertaking—has a rational underpinning.

Throughout the play, the entanglement of global thought systems continues to reveal itself in multiple ways. I will offer one more example. Building on the theme sparked by Anscombe's words, I am drawn to the ways in which Wright's hybridization of Catholic thought places *Lemma*—and much of his work—within a neo-Baroque register. That is, Wright's characters inhabit subject positions that re-code Christian tropes within indigenous belief systems that predated the arrival of Spanish and Portuguese colonizers to the lands now known as Mesoamerica and South America. Early in the play, Fuadach wryly

14 Probing deeper, we may also connect Forster to this trio by playing with the initials E. M., which appear in the poet's and the philosopher's names.

cites Luke 1:77–79, "to give light to those who sit in darkness and the shadow of death, to guide our way into the way of peace." Wright's character attributes the words to a "fraudulent physician," a moniker that summons the apostle's credentials at the same time as it dismisses the doctor's ability. Whatever ills Luke may have been capable of healing through medicine, his religious balm would not bring either light or peace to the inhabitants of the country now called Mexico. Each of *Lemma*'s characters is a mixture of Christian/Catholic beliefs and some other religious mode of knowing. This "other" quality does not, however, bar the characters from accessing the sacred.

The "other" quality of the hybrid sacred system of knowing demonstrated throughout *Lemma* is akin to the direct or gnostic experience of God familiar to mystics. This claim carries weight when we examine the final of Wright's six direct citations, which comes from the mystic Nicholas of Cusa's *De visione Dei* (1453): "I will attempt to lead you, by way of experiencing, through very simple and very common means, into a sacred darkness." If we juxtapose Cusa's words with those of Luke, we notice a similarity that quickly gives way to a crucial difference. The familiar trope of light and dark plays out in both quotations, but only Cusa's words retain a hold in *Lemma*'s territory, for only they elucidate the true fusion of light and dark. For Luke, heathens remain in the dark until the light is brought to them. For Cusa, personal experience of God leads to direct knowledge of the sacred without a shepherd. That direct knowledge takes place within "sacred darkness," a kind of plenitudinous emptiness discovered by hollowing out or decreating the self and becoming inhabited by the divine. As Forster's dancing body needed to bring life to the choreography of historic knowledge, Cusa's mystic body is required, but negatively; it is required to be emptied out and utilized as a point of view by God. Wright, no doubt aware of the theatricality of this arrangement, brings Cusa and Luke into the agon of *Lemma* and requires bodies of performers to step into the portals prepared by the text and the characters. In particular, these characters work within a religious framework common in what is termed Latin America, thereby placing Wright's mystic-theatrical experience in conversation with the neo-Baroque subjectivities discussed by authors including Alejo Carpentier, Carlos Fuentes, Haroldo de Campos, and Severo Sarduy.[15]

MUSICAL DRAMATURGY

Moving through the web of thought revealed by Wright's assembly of textual citations brings us into contact with the playwright's deep, diverse reservoir of knowledge. We find ourselves attempting to produce understanding out of a precise entanglement of analytic philosophy, mystic theology, geometric diagrams, linguistic polysemy, and the music without which we would not be able to feel the movement of the piece as a whole. *Lemma* revolves around a quality of musical dramaturgy that connects Wright to the jazz aesthetic of the Black Arts Movement while also placing him in his own sonic territory.

Throughout *Lemma*, the Lydian mode catches our ears. For example, Bricco, having volunteered to handle the vibrant white garment, attempts to prove his worthiness by singing a Lydian scale. Fuadach, both impressed and perturbed, responds, "Well, bravo for you."[16] Later, near the end of the play's action, the characters work to find the proper

---

15 Neo-baroque subjectivities are constructed through playful invention forced upon each subject by colonizing forces. The discipline of the colonizing impulse metastasizes into a brand of excess that frequently finds expression in works of art. Regarding the authors listed here, please see the following for examples: Alejo Carpentier, *Concierto barroco* (Mexico City: Siglo Veintiuno, 1974); Carlos Fuentes, "Elogio del barroco," *Boletín de la Biblioteca de Menéndez Pelayo* 69 (1993): 387–410; Haroldo de Campos, "The Rule of Anthropophagy: Europe under the Sign of Devoration," trans. Maria Wolff Tai, *Latin American Literary Review* 14, no. 27 (1986): 42–60; Severo Sarduy, "The Baroque and the Neobaroque" (1972), in *Baroque New Worlds: Representation, Transculturation, Counterconquest*, eds. Lois Parkinson Zamora and Monika Kaup (Durham, NC: Duke University Press, 2010), 270–291.

16 Wright, *Selected Plays*, vol. 1, 229.

rhythm that will lead to authentically executing the ritual dance necessary to achieve the knowledge they seek. Fuadach offers to play a primary part in the ritual, but Spalla, the other female character in the play, hesitates. "Bravo. But you haven't convinced me that you have learned to dance." Wright inserts a stage direction, "Fuadach sings the Lydian scale," and then Fuadach asks "Will that do?"[17] His singing is not enough, however; to give proper shape to the ensemble's composition, the characters all need to sing together or they will "lose this moment." After this decision, the actors repeat the opening stage direction of the performance.

What follows in the text is a repetition of the Voices, each assigned a specific set of lines to sing. These are the same lines offered as "prologues" in the beginning of the piece. Here, however, Wright affixes a name, and also a body, to each of the voices. Voice d lands in the body of Bacán. Voice e lands in Spalla. Bricco in Voice c. After reciting the text from the play's beginning, the characters collectively approach the edge of the third hour and do their best to conjure the memory of Elzbieta and Carmen into the theater. After a few pages of dialogue, a Musician enters. This new character, who appears only at the play's end, serves as a kind of choir master and arranges the bodies into one final configuration upon the stage:

> I want you to test your unadorned voices. [*Once he has them rearranged, he skips among them cajoling and assigning scales.*] From D to D octave, from E to E octave, from F to F octave, from G to G octave, from A to A octave, from C to C. You see that you can do this, can't you? Sure, you can. We all have our voices; we all have something a voice must address, or even tame.

As another stage direction tells us, "He points at each one for the assigned scale, then draws each one into singing a separate mode at the same time." While the characters sing, the Musician takes the white garment and dances away. The audience hears another voice draw

17 Wright *Selected Plays*, vol. 1, 234.

everything to a close: "There was a story that began with the usual drainage of certainties, but the tale was quickly delivered to the failing stars and propped upon inconceivable delight."[18]

The central role of singing, the presence of musical modes, and the repeated reference to the Lydian throughout the text brings to mind George Russell's work of music theory, *The Lydian Chromatic Concept of Tonal Organization* (1953). Russell's theory does not form a system, "but rather a view or philosophy of tonality in which the student, it is hoped, will find his identity."[19] This work instigated a paradigm shift in the sound of jazz improvisation and was championed by many well-known players, perhaps most assertively by Ornette Coleman. In an interview with Russell, Olive Jones provides a connection between Russell's work and Wright's play:

> Russell believes the significance of his concept to be that it puts music back on the track where it started back in the time of Pythagoras and other Greek philosophers. He feels that the problem has been that certain laws of Christianity influenced the development of music to such an extent that it was pulled away from its most natural systems toward the super-imminence of the major mode.... The Lydian Chromatic Concept reestablishes the link between the relatively recent laws of equal temperament and the ancient laws with their emphasis on movement through pure fifths.[20]

A musical historiographical maneuver in Russell's work rhymes boldly with Wright's aesthetic sensibilities. By uncovering the quality of sound and its related theoretical system from underneath the edifice erected on ancient grounds by the Christian church, Russell frees up a palette

18 *Selected Plays*, vol. 1, 239.

19 George Russell, *The Lydian Chromatic Concept of Tonal Organization*, vol. 1, *The Art and Science of Tonal Gravity*, 4th ed. (Brookline, MA: Concept, 2001). First published by the author in 1953.

20 Olive Jones and George Russell, "A New Theory for Jazz," *The Black Perspective in Music* 2, no. 1 (1974): 65.

of musical relationships that provides contemporary jazz musicians with a new kind of song, one capable of telling a story outside the harmonic and ideological constraints of the major mode.

Russell has always been vocal about the social relevance of his Lydian chromatic concept:

> it's o.k. to talk about black liberation and black this-and-that, but nothing is going to change fundamentally in this society which is ruled by laws that are so precious to their makers. One has to question the laws. That's what I did; that's what absorbs me.[21]

Musical laws penned by the church do not provide the conditions of possibility for a truly emancipatory musical language and expression. Likewise, laws touting equality will always harbor a principle of structural exclusion that makes of white people always-already deserving of equality and Black people always-almost-ready-to-deserve it. What would be needed for equality would be a completely new language with which to pronounce new laws premised on new ways of living together. Unable to swing that, Russell finds a new (old) language that eventually becomes the bedrock of so-called free jazz.

In the same way that Russell's theory provides musicians "with an awareness of the full spectrum of tonal colors available in the equal temperament tuning," Wright's global web of entangled knowledge systems presents theater makers with a synesthetic fusion of sight and sound capable of producing a theater space that doubles as a site of ritual incantation. *Lemma* is a score from which players might produce a precise set of time-space coordinates that guide the performers and audiences to the cusp of the always-becoming present, an event horizon that leads not to firm identities and certain knowledge calculated in advance but, rather, to a fluid and improvisatory identity of both things and people. The text attempts to paint a wormhole into existence through its music, one capable of reviving memory and honoring the capacities of the "American" identity (understood here in its

21 Jones and Russell, "A New Theory for Jazz," 72.

neo-Baroque, *mestizaje* shape). Similar to Wright's recently published *The Geometry of Rhythm* (2019), in which two characters explore a process of inter-subjective becoming keyed to the movement of the so-called "Gypsy" or Harmonic Minor Scale, *Lemma* produces a visual event (theater) from a musical dramaturgy that departs from the tonal potentialities inhering within the Lydian mode.

WRIGHT'S LEMMA

The play's name is a polyseme. A lemma in the discourse of logic is a passage forged through a minor proposition en route to a decisive proof. In lexicography, a lemma is the "canonical form" from which issues a set of related words (e.g., dance: dance, dances, danced, dancing). Psycholinguists use "lemma" to name the abstract concept of a word that the brain selects prior to uttering anything, a kind of mental model from which will sprout a sound laden with meaning. With Wright's play, we find a new valence to "lemma." The text is a transition point, a hinge, or perhaps a port of embarkation that doubles as a cellular matrix from which grows both potential and actual lives (which always contain pasts, presents, and futures). *Lemma* takes place at the horizon where a memory is given form through the precise language and musicality with which that memory is spoken. We might be able to claim that the memory in question is a history of love and death, generally, spoken of through the particular story of the sisters Elzbieta and Carmen. This history informs the identity of the characters in the present. Indeed, each is incomplete without the memory. At the same time, each character will remain precisely incomplete because the memory's repeated telling ensures no static identity for the figures and events that make up the past. *Lemma*, with its emphasis on the art of arrangement through which an individual makes him/her/themself out of the memories and texts of others, becomes legible as a passage, one that connects past and present in the unfolding of theatrical action.

To make a self within that passage, we must dance in a rhythm that allows the multiplicity within us to come forward in harmony, where "harmony" is a free(r) concept that eludes the constraints of the binary of harmony/dissonance. *Lemma* shows us the labor required of bodies attempting to find this rhythm. Here, it becomes possible to speak of Wright's lemma as a study in rhythm, and more specifically of idiorrhythm.

This strange term comes from Roland Barthes's 1977 lectures at the Collège de France, translated into English as *How to Live Together*. The word has Ancient Greek origins and comes from the fusion of *idios* (particular) and *rhuthmos* (rhythm, though in a particular sense, as I will explain), and belongs, historically, to "any [religious] community that respects each individual's own personal rhythm."[22] It was, therefore, on the other side of the disciplinary continuum from what would become the Christian monasteries, insofar as the latter mandated a strict rhythm in accordance with a temporal scheme constructed around prayer and a long list of representational practices that bound individual monks to the larger body of the church. From this word, idiorrhythm, Barthes develops a typology of communities, most clearly apparent in works of fiction, presenting multiple ways of living with each other. The tacit "we" here is quite global in reach, and thus we might read Barthes's lectures as a philosophical fantasy aimed at conjuring a utopian space through art. Barthes's conjuring skills are limited, however, insofar as no utopia pops into existence. Nevertheless, the thinking demonstrated in the lecture series prepares "idiorrhythm" for a wide variety of uses in philosophical discourse.

In terms of *Lemma*, we find the six primary characters engaged in an idiorrhythmic exercise. Their incessant work of arranging themselves properly, attempting to locate "the proper and perfect configuration of their group," is precisely a syncopation of particular rhythms. They never fall in line with a single commanding rhythm, despite the hope that such a master rhythm will accomplish a performance of the play's ritual. Instead, we see each of the characters assert his or her own

22 Claude Coste, quoted by Roland Barthes in *How to Live Together: Novelistic Simulations of Some Everyday Spaces*, trans. Kate Briggs (New York: Columbia University Press, 2013), xxii.

mode of speech, philosophical inclinations, and styles of movement. Only when the Musician arrives at the conclusion of the play does the group seem to find their perfect configuration, but even then the arrangement permits heterogeneity. Each character sings his or her own scale. The scales overlap into a cosmological concert in which the particularity of the character evades complete subsumption into the group, much in the same way that a sextet of jazz instrumentalists can collaborate as a group, find a jam, yet never fully cohere into a homogeneous singularity.

The purpose of summoning idiorrhythm in this essay, however, has as much to do with Wright as a poet and historiographer as it does with the world of the play he has created. Barthes, in the lecture section from February 2, 1977, dedicated to "power," offers the following insight:

> Once again, what we're dealing with is: a consubstantial relationship between power and rhythm. Before anything else, the first thing that power imposes is a rhythm (to everything: a rhythm of life, of time, of thought, of speech). The demand for idiorrhythm is always made in opposition to power.[23]

Let's return to the question I posed at the start of this essay: Where is Wright? He was not in step with the rhythm of the Black Arts Movement, as it was the arm of the Black Power Movement, a movement committed to producing a single Black Power that could counter deathly Whiteness. Despite their revolutionary gestures (both successful and failed attempts), both BAM and the Black Power Movement more generally sought to impose *a* rhythm on Black thought. But Wright's affinity for idiorrhythmic structures carried him off elsewhere. More specifically, both then and now, he understands the Americas to operate as an idiorrhythmic experiment. As such, the America for which he produces space in his poetry and his plays combines so many voices and cultural traditions into a heterogenous assemblage that preserves

23 Barthes, *How to Live Together*, 35.

the friction between disparate knowledge systems while also demonstrating how difference can cohabitate with itself. In this way, Wright's *rhuthmos* rhymes with the aesthetics of the neo-Baroque and the jazz improvisations imagined by Russell, Coleman, and other musicians of a similar ilk.

Just as Russell sought to bypass the harmonic laws imposed by the Christian church so as to revive for modern jazz the philosophical world of music alive in Pythagoras's era, so too can we bypass the church of the Black Arts Movement to situate Wright in a historical trajectory that cultivates the Americas out of a radically heterogeneous combination of sources. To do this, we can borrow Barthes's distinction between rhythm and *rhuthmos*:

> rhythm ≠ *rhuthmos*. Idiorrythmy: a means of safeguarding *rhuthmos*, that is to say a flexible, free, mobile rhythm; a transitory, fleeting form, but a form nonetheless.... *Rhuthmos*: a rhythm that allows for approximation, for imperfection, for a supplement, a lack, an *idios*: what doesn't fit the structure, or would have to be made to fit.[24]

Characters attempt to figure out how to live together. They arrange themselves like notes in a scale and like atoms in a molecule, attempting to find the right fit. Their movements are supported by the certainties of historical voices but they also remain tethered to the uncertainties of memory. As such, there is always a lack or an imperfection in their arrangements. Wright is jamming here, and his own idiorrhythmic sensibilities provide the overall tone of the jam session. Whatever we make of *Lemma*, we must preserve the act of making, showcasing that as a vital element to this work for the theater.

WHAT HISTORIOGRAPHY BECOMES?

Throughout Wright's work, poiesis produces strands in the great web of the world while also revealing the fact that entanglement was always already taking place. *Lemma* produces a different Black, American

24 Barthes, *How To Live Together*, 35.

theater. What I am able to present of the play's ritual conjuration and jazz structure in this essay offers a soundbite of an idiorrhythmic community of intellectual forces bodied forth in characters with their own particular aims and desires. We see here a glimpse of the multitude that might thrive in all of us who identify as Americans if we broaden the scope of our identity to include practices and harmonies that have been occluded by dominant narratives of belonging. At the same time, Wright is simply showing us what already exists. Anscombe, Donne, Russell, the Lydian mode, the sound of the *agogo*, rituals hinging on the swift blade of an obsidian knife: these atoms combine into the ever-transforming molecules of American lives. The question is: Do we hear all these sounds when we speak of a "we"?

Lemma presents a specific set of historiographic maneuvers challenging three key aspects of contemporary thinking related to theater and performance studies. First, by staging his thought in theatrical form, Wright destabilizes the notion that both historical knowledge and historiographic consciousness in the present are ever readymade or complete. Throughout the drama's development, the perpetual arrangement of characters presents identities *in formation*. Likewise, the ritual frame subtending the play's action provides a repeatable structure but demands of the performers, like most theater, that they enact the play's action live, as if playing a concert. I understand Wright's lesson here as one that addresses the processual development of what things are. Things come to be. Nothing already is. The theater that houses *Lemma* is not one that pre-exists the staging of the play but comes into existence instead as the play is produced. Likewise, the past, any past of which historiographers speak, does not pre-exist the telling, and thus the inflection of the telling and the arrangement of notes effectively construct the past while also shaping and reshaping it in the present.

Second, the relationship between the identities of *Lemma*'s characters and their memories and histories challenges me to rethink the way historiographers drag the present into the past and represent past events in the present. Perhaps one reason that Wright's characters never fully or successful reconstruct the central past event of the play's action—i.e., the disappearance of the three sisters—is because that past event is always in flux. As such, without an objective and static past from which to draw any certainties, the characters in the present get hung up on how they are *playing* the past, so to speak. In terms of historiography, the parallel is clear. In the absence of a static and certain past event or a timeless space safely housing historical objects and personages, don't we always find a field of tensions produced each time that the present attempts to make contact with the past? Remembering correctly may not be possible, but the ethics of remembering *in tune* are nevertheless palpable. To play the past is to reveal how the past gathers concretely in the present, if even only temporarily before shifting form. Historiography thus takes shape as a spatial undertaking, not a science undertaking the revelation of temporal mysteries, but an art producing theatrical experiments in the present, the purpose of which is to examine the tensions between diverse thought systems shaping each and every historical figure, object, and event.

Third, any such identity must never succumb to the illusion that it emerges from a single original point. Black American theater is assembled each time a specific palette of relationships is activated. In the case of the Black Arts Movement, that palette had only a certain number of colors. All paintings were to be created from that color scheme, or else the resulting product would not and could not serve the movement. Wright is clearly unconcerned with such service. Rather, we find him several decades into a deep dig that has unearthed a surprisingly heterogeneous and at times dissonant tonal and chromatic matrix. Robert Graves and John Donne participate in Wright's American identity, but so too does Russell's music theory and Cavafy's uneasy Greek poetic inheritance. Ancient Greek drama provides a productive sense of communal or collective voicing. Beckett's contemporary uptake of Irish aesthetic sensibilities is in play, too. Spanish becomes a fruitful language through which to voice some of this aesthetic. Wright hears all of these sources and linguistic forms in the sound of the *agogo* and other instruments brought to the New World by enslaved Africans.

He wonders what types of rhythms will be of use as Americans dance their way into existence. Could we say that the adjective "Black" takes a backseat to American in *Lemma*? Yes, but only insofar as the latter constitutes a theater in itself through which all the tensions of Blackness, and for that matter Whiteness, will play out and arrange themselves into ever-shifting and uncertain identities.

CODE: A SPORT (APPROACHING JAY WRIGHT)

Preface

Duriel E. Harris

CODE: A SPORT is an evolving theatrical project emerging into form through encounter with Jay Wright's plays *Passage* and *Lemma* and resonant conceptual mindscapes. Intrigued by the potential depth and breadth of a companion volume to Jay Wright's plays and the prospect of explicitly situating my work in this contemplative field, I readily accepted the invitation to participate in this adventure.

Having first read poems by Jay Wright soon after college, I remembered them as enigmatic, mystical, curious, and often puzzling tight philosophical packages that kept me pondering for hours at a time. What would the plays be like? Where would they take me? What different modes of thinking and listening would I be compelled to consider?

Collaboration is a key component of my creative practice, so I journeyed forth, delighting in *withness*,[a] excited by the opportunity to

[a] The endeavor to release the analytical tendency to "think against," learned throughout my years in the academy, and instead take up withness as primary mode of creative-critical practice was inspired by sustained interaction with poet Lisa Samuels. Other instances of withness informing my engagement with Wright's *Lemma* and *Passage* include engagements with: Will Daddario's "*Lemma*: Jay Wright's Idiorrhythmic American Theater" (2021); Paul Laurence Dunbar's *Sport of the Gods* (1902); Lyn Hejinian's "Some Notes Toward a Poetics" (2009); Iayze's "556 (Green Tip)" (2022); Mankwe Ndosi's "Sassy Ragdale Lindy" (2017); interviews with Sun Ra, via Robert Mugge's *Sun Ra: A Joyful Noise* (1980); Joan Retallack's *The Poethical Wager* (2003); Daniel Sack's "Introduction" to *Imagined Theatres: Writing for a Theoretical Stage* (2017); SpotemGottem's "Beat Box (feat. Young M.A) (Freestyle)" (2021) and conversations with YWWG Screenwriters (2021–2023).

foreground provocative shared muses/musings in the theater (read play space as in playground, park, garden) and auditorium (read concert hall, sanctuary, acoustic marvel, temple) of my imagination.

I thought I might compose a short sound experiment, a lyric essay, or series of prose poems to contribute to the volume. However it would be, I made a commitment to my bodyself to luxuriate in sound, wonder, sensation, shadows, silences, roots and reaches, serious play and all manner of quirky writerly inclinations in an organic process of composition: "Breathe-in experience, / breathe-out poetry" or whatever being (being being) made, making manifest.[β] And also deepening, revisiting, re-searching, re-sounding, re-envisioning, toward a full realization of the project.

In so doing, a breaking open. And a full-length play in progress.

Approaching Jay Wright, writing alongside *Passage* and *Lemma*, a series of concerns surface and remain, alternately illuminating the field of play: How do the rhythms of human embodiment and verbal language structure meaning-making in the instantiation of theater? How does the matter/material of human subjectivity evolve in relationship to vibration, space, and energy? How does the ritual enactment of theater augment the occasion of the work—the working out and working through—through evolving phases (versions, variations, riffs) of creation? How is the core substance of the sacred distilled and made manifest in the imagination made real in play, in utterance, in encounter?

β In the moment of writing, Muriel Rukeyser's description of poesis/poetic impulse surfaced in memory as a fitting approximation of the generative phases of my ongoing process of developing "Code: A Sport" during this sustained engagement with Wright's plays (*Lemma* most especially) in what I experience as a vast envelope of encounter.

CODE: A SPORT (APPROACHING JAY WRIGHT)

A Drama

Duriel E. Harris

"[W]hat do dreams know of boundaries?"
—Amelia Earhart

THE PLAYERS

BLEVIN (AKA TRASH GIRL, WOLF, RAZOR, BOX WINE) An office cleaner, aspiring visual artist. A black vegan leather choker collar with a Black Sun aka sun wheel (Sonnenrad) pendant is affixed to her neck.

SU (AKA SMUSH FACE SU, AUTOCORRECT) A grifter, squatter, aspiring writer. In a black fanny pack she carries a small power bank and a discontinued older model smartphone in a faux cassette tape case.

BAGO (AKA DINO BAGO, BAGOROCKS) An ambitious, aspiring entrepreneur. A pristine blue folder containing his business plan is his prized possession. His fingernails are painted black.

BRODY (AKA THE QUEEN BRODY) A radical activist, aspiring scholar. He displays 3 prominent black ink tattoos: A lowercase Greek letter lambda (λ), a Double male symbol (⚣, double interlocking Mars symbol) and a Pansexual symbol(⚤, a P symbol with arrow and cross tail). His tagline is: A buffoon and a murder.

MARLOWE (AKA MARLOWE, A CAT) An ambitious undercover AI who appears in the form of a golden-eyed, dark brown furred, talking Maine coon domestic cat.

THE HIVE (AKA THE FOUNDATION) A Hive Mind (chorus) sponsor of cutting-edge clean energy research. CEO of H.I.V.E Foundation.

[LET THE GAME BEGIN]

[SETTING: *A green valley. In a small clearing of a 20-acre tract of overgrown, wooded farmland, sits a squat, ranch-style white clapboard house. Behind the house, a one-room white clapboard church. Behind the church, a small cemetery with a dozen black granite headstones. Behind the cemetery, a nest the size of a small car. The nest is a blank space, a soft darkness surrounded by sticks and branches and bits of wool and oilcloth.*

At the far end, farthest from the house, near the nest edge, four rusted folding metal chairs are arranged as if in conversation but subtly cheating out toward the foothills of a blue mountain range. The mountains are twisted as if turning away from the valley, shunning the house and its occupants who languish in the wide but sparsely furnished rooms. The living room is starkly lit with blank black walls reminiscent of the matte stage floor of a black box college theater. There is a small, overturned rowboat behind a secondhand sofa. Even with the shapes and sounds of people in it, the house seems empty. Suddenly A CAT.]

MARLOWE, A CAT: [*in the style of soliloquy*] Words are the most powerful drug used by humankind? Meh. The idea of language as a "drug" and even the concept of the drug itself is passé. Non-naturally occurring substances or naturally occurring substances employed by an outside agent to impact a certain alteration of consciousness or bodily systems, etc., etc. From my vantage point I'd advise us to entertain the full scope of the human body, the reach of its mechanisms.

But we're getting ahead of ourselves. There is a run of show and I am off script.

Welcome to our drama, our game. I am Marlowe, A Cat. You are the witnesses. Together, dear panel, we must judge tonight's contestants. Once they realize you are there, they will each attempt to sway you to their cause, to befriend you to undo the threat they imagine you cast upon them. I know you are no more real or powerful than they but how for such as these does wisdom weigh against desire and fear? They'll shake their fists at passersby to distract themselves from their closing throats, speedy hearts, and sweaty palms. In the hours when they quit their banter you can hear their queasy stomachs' jittery flipping. Such purple and majestic mountains they will climb to reach you. Such sour, sullen valleys and rivers they'll traverse, sadly leaving their bodies for another day, a year, a score or two. However long the tubing lasts. [*beat*] Oh sweets! I said drama, didn't I? We're less feeble together. We begin! Keep up!

[CURTAINS OPEN TO REVEAL: A SCENE!]

[MARLOWE *draws us into the living room where* BLEVIN *sits on one end of a bulky second-hand sofa, drawing with one of an array of dark colored pencils on a fat white sketch pad.* SU *sits on the other end of the sofa, staring at a mobile phone screen.* BAGO *sits, within* SU*'s reach, cross legged on the floor at the coffee table, in front of the sofa looking at dogeared papers in a blue folder. Just beyond* BLEVIN*'s feet, close to a bay window,* BRODY *lies on his belly on an area rug reading a comic book.* MARLOWE *walks around them exploring the room, then stops at the bay window and stares out intently. Quite suddenly* MARLOWE *begins licking the backs of their paws and rubbing them on their face as if to wash it.*]

BLEVIN: [*to* MARLOWE] What were you doing at the window? Has someone come to save us? I saw something, too. Look, I drew it here. [*long pause*] Marlowe, are you ignoring me again?

MARLOWE: [*to* BRODY] If it pleases you, Your Majesty, tell us the snow story.

BRODY: Ugh. Not now.

MARLOWE: [*twirling across the floor*] Snow! Snow! Snow! Snow! Snow! Snow! Snow! Snow!…

BRODY: [*silences* MARLOWE*'s chanting*] *Seriously,* Marlowe? That's what has us stuck here, with them! [*points at* BLEVIN *and* SU]

MARLOWE: They cannot help that they are girls. That is the fault of their mothers and fathers. Mostly their fathers.

BRODY: Do stop twirling before you hurt yourself.

SU: Or spin like a top and crash into the walls. Swing from the rafters by your tail. Start a fire. Do something interesting.

BRODY: Mean, petulant girls.

SU: I'm bored. You freaks are boring.

BLEVIN: [*looks up from her drawing*] You're boring. Why don't you go kill yourself, name-brand?

SU: Fuck off.

BLEVIN: You wish.

BAGO: [*puts papers inside blue folder, closes it with finality*] Brody, wanna smoke? It's pretty good stuff. You, too, Marlowe, if you want.

[*A screened in porch appears.* BAGO, BRODY, *and* MARLOWE *retreat to it and smoke*]

SU: [*mocking* BAGO] I have a blue folder! [*beat*] So, Trash Girl, what did you see?

BLEVIN: Oh, Autocorrect, wouldn't you like to know?

SU: We can't do this forever. Who knows how long we're stuck here together? The boys are getting along. We girls have to stick together. [*beat*] Like how I did that?

BLEVIN: Yeah. Nifty. [*beat*] OK. Flip for it.

SU: Let's see... [SU *tries a back flip. Fails.*]

BLEVIN: Wow. Smush Face, some cheerleader you are.

SU: Don't call me that. And I'd like to see you try it.

BLEVIN: I'm not that kind.

SU: Well what kind are you?

BLEVIN: Do you want to see or not? [BLEVIN *shows* SU *the drawing*]

SU: Oh shit. That's dark, that's fucked up. You saw that, out there? Fuck. We're fucked. We're fucked!

BLEVIN: Yeah. Well. At least this is not a pissy basement.

SU: I want to go home.

BLEVIN: Have at it, Schmauto. Call your daddy to come rescue us. Oh, I forgot you're already dead to him.

SU: You're a bitch. Why do I even like you?

BLEVIN: You don't. You're just lonely.

[BAGO, BRODY, *and* MARLOWE *return from the porch and form a chorus line just behind the sofa, giggling about everything and nothing, obviously high*]

BAGO: [*to* SU, *mimicking Missy Elliot performance*] Is that your bitch???

[BAGO, BRODY, *and* MARLOWE *burst out laughing and pointing, they dance to a rap song playing in their heads.* SU *stomps off, past them, past the porch, into a yawning darkness.*]

BLEVIN: [*moves away from the sofa*] Y'all stupid.

MARLOWE: [*waits a beat, then turns to follow* SU] Su is sensitive. I should check on her.

BAGO
BRODY } [*in unison, laughing*] Whatever.
MARLOWE

MARLOWE: [*soberly*] But really. Duty calls.

[MARLOWE *trots off, following* SU. *Suddenly, there is a flash of light, everything goes black and* MARLOWE *reappears outside of the living room, within reach of the audience, at the lip of an abyss, the chasm between worlds.*]

MARLOWE: [*to audience, their confidantes*] Like how I did that? I'm full of tricks. By design. You've met the players' semi-public faces, now meet their skeletons.

[*The living room reappears with a coffee table full of snacks.* BLEVIN *stands at the window.* BAGO *and* BRODY *sit on the sofa stuffing their faces, gulping soda pop, and chewing with their mouths open.*]

BLEVIN: [*staring into the darkness beyond the window pane*] I don't trust that cat. "Service and Support Companion," my flat white ass.

BRODY: They are as trustworthy as any of us.

BLEVIN: Exactly. And why go after Su.

BRODY: [*slices a thin line across his throat tracing a memory*] Sharps.

BLEVIN: Hmph. Interesting.

BAGO: [*to* BRODY] Wait. Is she a tagger? That's awesome!

BRODY: Sharps! You know, razor blades, scissors, knives…

BAGO: [*to* BRODY] Ohhhhhh.

BLEVIN: [*chuckling*] An event to cut the monotony.

BRODY: Wow. You really are a bitch. A flat-white-ass trailer trash bitch.

BLEVIN: Tell me something I don't know, Queen B. Why else would I sign up for this shit show? Best train out of Dodge. "Ambitious, recent college grads wanted for year-long paid study." Free travel, free lodging, free meals. "Come unplug at our 2,000-acre lakeside property." Luxury accommodations. Plus studio space. Private beach. Mountain trails. Chef. $10K signing bonus up front. In my bank account a month in advance. I mean, I paid off a loan. What's not to like? Well, Scam-I-am, here's to the too-good bait and switch: Come get packed into a driverless car with two scrots, a tortured half-breed lesbian, and a talking cat. Come get trapped in Nowhere Valley in a blizzard in the middle of May! "The Property" is a shit bush. If I wanted to lounge in a musty prefab house deep in America's ass crack with clueless fuck-turds and no internet, I'd have just stayed home.

BRODY: Potty mouth much, Miss Congeniality? Besides, you signed the waiver and the NDA. We all did.

BLEVIN: Don't remind me. Buzzkill list of regrets. I need a drink.

BRODY: Yeah, Bago, my high is toast.

BAGO: [*perks up*] First we need pizza. And beer. And maybe bratwurst. And a bottle for Blevin.

BLEVIN: It speaks!

BAGO: Or a box. These nuts, Trash Girl.

BLEVIN: Witty! Typical frat boy fashion.

BRODY: OK kids, quit whining. This situation is temporary. The Foundation is sending another ride. Marlowe said the car transmitted the coordinates immediately. We'll be at The Property soon and this detour will be a distant memory. We just have to wait this out. Pizza and beer sound great, Bago. As soon as Marlowe gets back.

BAGO: I'm going to the blue room to nap. Beauty sleep. [BAGO *grabs his darling folder, smacks it against the back of* BLEVIN's *head, and retreats into a sliver of blue smoke. His voice is a buoy in hazy silence.*] With that mug you must stay awake all night, wolf spawn.

BLEVIN: Just so I can haunt your dreams, numb-nuts. [*beat*] I can't see shit out there. But I have a bad feeling. Something wicked this way comes. And I need a drink before it gets here. Where is that bottle?

BRODY: It's only 10 AM, park princess, try giving your liver a break.

BLEVIN: How do you know what time it is?

BRODY: Clock. [*points to wall*]

BLEVIN: Then it's been 10 AM for 3 days. I'm telling you: rotten in Denmark.

BRODY: Broken clock does not equal foul play.

BLEVIN: Tequila.

BRODY: Alcoholic.

BLEVIN: I'm not an alcoholic. Alcoholics go to meetings.

BRODY: Nice T-shirt. You skipped the big reveal: You're "not an alcoholic." You're "a drunk."

BLEVIN: Fine. I'm a drunk. Now hand over that 1800 Reposada Tequila, Chiquita Banana, pronto before our sitter returns.

BRODY: You're not an invalid—yet. Get it yourself.

[*The screened-in porch appears.* BLEVIN *leaves her post at the window to retreat to it. The porch disappears as soon as she arrives, seemingly swallowing her.* BRODY *pulls out a catalog hidden beneath him under the sofa seat cushion. He opens it expectantly. Stares at it intently.*]

BRODY: [*studying catalog pages*] Ooo, sweet child of mine.

BLEVIN: [*from a far corner of the porch*] Where is it?

BRODY: Overhead.

BLEVIN: [*farther*] Where, Brody?

BRODY: Highest shelves. Ladder.

BLEVIN: [*farther in*] For Christsakes!

BRODY: [*laughing*] Work for your food, Miss Thing.

BLEVIN: [*an echo*] There's nothing here!!

BRODY: Other side! [*beat*]

BLEVIN: [.] Ohh! My lord, what a morning!

BRODY: Jackpot!

BLEVIN: I'm going to chill out here for a minute.

BRODY: I bet. [BRODY *flips through last pages of catalog. Mops his brow. Stuffs catalog back under the seat cushion. Lifts the edges of the rug under the coffee table. Begins to slide out another catalog, changes his mind. Sits back, fades into the sofa, closes his eyes and breathes very deeply, as if meditating.*]

[SCENE!]

[*In the church interior, front pews. Both* SU *and* MARLOWE *kneel facing the altar*]

SU: Thanks for sitting with me.

MARLOWE: Sure.

SU: I need to confess something, Marlowe.

MARLOWE: What is it, Su?

SU: First, I'm sorry. I shouldn't have said those things to you. I don't want anything to happen to you.

MARLOWE: I know.

SU: Do you accept my apology? Do you forgive me?

MARLOWE: Yes, of course.

SU: Thank you. That means a lot.

MARLOWE: Yes. I know. Is there something else?

SU: Maybe you can tell. I'm struggling. I stopped taking my meds. To do the study. I didn't want to lie on the forms, so I stopped. Flat out. I think I need to go back.

MARLOWE: Back on the meds?

SU: Back somewhere. I can't go back home. My father stopped speaking to me when I told him I was bi. Just never said another word. Next time I came back from college to visit I found everything from my room in bins in the garage. All of my stuff. House looked like I never lived there. Literally like I was never there. He just erased me. Like he had erased my mother and my twin brother, Kendall. I went from princess to ghost. I should have known it was coming.

My brother might be dead. I don't know. I can't feel him anymore.

He walked out of the house one day. Kept walking. Usually we'd just ride it out at the park but not that day. It felt different.

Kendall had had an argument with dad about, I don't know, our bikes on the lawn, popsicles, the screen door. It was the summer we turned twelve. Every afternoon it was the same. Dad yelling down Kendall's throat and Kendall taking it, clenching his jaw, clenching his fists. Then dad going in on our mom, with his regular taunts saying Kendall was "a little punk ass half-white pink bastard" and "more bitch than the no good halfwhite whore he fell out of who'd rather turn tricks than take care of her kids."

She tried to take us with her but he said he'd hunt her down and send her to meet Jesus. I'll never forget the sound she made when he said that.

My mother left in her nightgown in a taxi. He wouldn't even let her get dressed. We waved her goodbye from the window. Everyone was crying. He said we were his kids and he'd kill anybody who tried taking us. Then one after the other he treated us like shit. Like you keep an old dog to have somebody to kick.

And, of course, he's the sheriff. Top cop in town.

I tried calling my mom at the number I have for my grandpa but it rings a senior center in Idaho. They said he doesn't live there and they don't know how to help me, have I tried Boise City Hall for records. That was a dead end. Last I knew they were in Georgia, where my grandpa had a church. That was fifteen years ago.

So. I don't have anywhere to go now that school is out. I gave away all my shit. All I have left is this dead phone, whatever's in my bag at the house, and 150 bucks. No apartment. No one checking for me. Blevin is right. I'm so lonely. Tired. [*beat*] I can't stop thinking about it.

MARLOWE: About cutting?

SU: About the schedule I made last year. For post-graduation. For when the money runs out. I have four plans. One for each weekday Monday through Thursday.

MARLOWE: Monday through Thursday?

SU: So someone will find me. Before I stink.

[MARLOWE *lies down, leans their head on* SU, *purrs.* SU *strokes their fur, speaks with renewed sharp and crisp articulation.*]

I don't think I can make it to The Property. I'm so tired of pretending to be brave, pretending to be badass. Us being stuck here. Together. The energy. Mean. Tearing at you. Jibes. Jabs. Can't drop my guard. And no real outlet, no sanctuary. At least not for me. Not even sleep. I can't write anything, haven't written in weeks. My notepad might as well be a brick. And no real conversations just catty quips. Oh. My bad. Not you. No offense.

MARLOWE: None taken.

SU: I just. I need to be there—at The Property—now or not at all.

[MARLOWE *lifts their head, looks around the church. Stands, stretches to their full length—it seems they have gotten longer, more muscular, more fierce looking since their first speech.* MARLOWE *purrs, framing their words with a palpable energy, nudges* SU *to stand and calmly walks out of the church toward the cemetery and the nest.* SU *follows.*]

MARLOWE: Let's go for a walk. Smoke?

[*A flash of light. A plume of smoke. A shadow arises from the cemetery, passes over the church, settles into the house where, in the living room,* BRODY, BLEVIN, *and* BAGO *sit like chums on the sofa, sleeping. Even with the three asleep, smiling in their common dream, spines softening into the sofa, the vibe of the house takes on a steelier edge. Abruptly,* BAGO *snores, waking the other two, then himself.* MARLOWE *stands by the window licking their paws as if to clean their face.*]

MARLOWE: The Foundation says another car is coming. And a tow. Within the hour.

BLEVIN: Finally! Fuck!

BRODY: Yes. I feel refreshed and we'll soon be back on the road.

[BRODY *joins* MARLOWE *at the window*]

We're certain to appreciate our luxury digs even more having had this detour, don't you think, Marlowe?

MARLOWE: As such, Your Majesty will now indulge us with the snow story.

BRODY: It is a good story.

BLEVIN: Mine was better.

BAGO: [*scratching himself, he laughs and pulls a bottle from his shorts*] A little bitter maybe, but not better.

BLEVIN: [*moving away from* BAGO] How would you know? You can barely read, frat boy. And, dude, brush your teeth. Your breath smells like a cow's ass.

MARLOWE: Mean drunk.

BRODY: Better to smell like a cow's ass than look like one, eh Trash Box? He can brush his teeth.

BLEVIN: I'll drink to that but we need another bottle.

BRODY: Now who can't read?

MARLOWE: The more you drink, the better they look.

BAGO: Yeah. Nothing a little tequila won't cure. And reading's overrated. I read maybe 4 books all 4 years of college. And look at me, I'm doing great!

BLEVIN: [*makes an X with her forearms, mimicking* Family Feud] Survey says?! *Anh!!!!*

MARLOWE: Oh so sour. [*beat*] Let's play a game. Kill some time and lighten the mood. Laughter is the best medicine.

BRODY: Like *Reader's Digest*. My great-grandpa Frank used to get those. Evil bastard.

BLEVIN: Family resemblance. So, Marlowe the Cat. What do you have in mind? Drinking game? Truth or Dare? Pin the Tail on the Dumbass?

MARLOWE: Something for everyone, especially you, Madam Wordsmith. A cypher.

BAGO: Yo! I'm down.

BLEVIN: Like rap?

BRODY: Ooooo! I'm all in. This should be good.

BAGO: I spit rhymes on a dime, from the dome into my phone. Yo! Ya heard!

BLEVIN: [*rhythmlessly*] Yo yo yo I'm a big dick baller, big shot caller, bigger and taller…Waste of breath.

BRODY: Ohhhh. The truth comes out. Shakespeare's sister is a poet not.

BLEVIN: What do you know about Shakespeare's sister?

BRODY: Don't be shocked. I was an English major for a semester. And we all graduated college.

BLEVIN: Fake news.

BRODY: Listen and weep.

BLEVIN: Sure. Fine. Whatever.

BRODY: Marlowe, beatbox?

MARLOWE: Of course!

BAGO: Bagorocks is like: "So much water on my neck it's like I'm detoxin, two drums and two sticks I'm beatboxin, eyyy!" Ya heard! Young M.A went in on that SpotemGottem joint. I love that shit! Classic!

BLEVIN: Do we really have to do this?

BRODY: Oh yes we must! It's time to take out the Trash.

BLEVIN: So clever.

BRODY: OK, Marlowe, do you. But basic.

MARLOWE: Right. Dialing it down, Your Highness. Let's try twelve bars.
Ready? Here we go! [*beatboxing*]

B-B-Buh Cah Tst-Tst-Tst

Buh Cah Tst-Tst-Tst

Buh Cah Tst-Tst-Tst

Wicki-wicki-wicki-wicki-wicki-wicki-wicki

B-Buh Cah Tst-Tst-Tst

B-Buh Cah-Buh-Tst-Tst-Tst

B-Buh Cah Tst-Tst-Tst

B-Buh Cah-Buh-Tst-Tst-Tst

[MARLOWE *continues beatboxing under the rhymes, pausing in between MCs*]

BAGO: Uh, yeah, Uh, yeah, Uh
I kill yo bitch like I kill this beat, yeah
No bait and switch bro, my shit is sweet, unh
You play the fool but we play for keeps, unh
Got a business plan but you know my heart is in the streets
I roll with hittas so just keep your beef, unh
I roll this blunt so I can keep the peace, unh
I roll with murda thugs and nasty freaks
Your mother ride my dick get that deep throat no teef
Your momma fine, son, that's a compliment
She ride it like I pro so I have no regrets
I pull out savage mode cause I got bands to get
Plus I'm high as superfly and I ain't landed yet

Ooooooo, Bagorocks bitches!!

BRODY
MARLOWE } [*in unison, astonished*] Oh shit!

BRODY: Dayyyyy-yyyyummmmm, MC Bagorocks born with the flow!

MARLOWE: Seasoned bars, indeed!

BRODY: Shakespeare? Or shall I? [*beat*] OK, it's me, it's me! Give me something fishy for the Ball, Marlowe. Something cunty, cunt-cunt for this pose.

MARLOWE: Certainly, Your Highness.

BRODY: Hey hey hey, mmh
Queen Brody here to read you, mmh
You look hungry let me feed you, what
We'll let you rhyme but we don't need you, nope
Open your mind, The Study freed you, right
So stop complaining you don't need to, hey
Cause Diva Brody's here to lead you, mmh
Do what he say and peep what he do, right
You failed the test you need a redo, wait
Don't back it up you'll break your T2, what
Heart trouble, darling? You should regroup, what
Get happy, drunk, they're giving free soup, what
And take the mic because the Queen's through!

Hey Hey Hey Bitch!

[BAGO *motions slamming the mic and flips the bird at* BLEVIN. MARLOWE *twirls and curtsies in approval.* BLEVIN *rolls her eyes.*]

BRODY: What, Trash Girl? No trash talking now?

BLEVIN: Really? That's it, Queen B? That's your rap?

BRODY: Well, what you got under that blonde wig? You've had enough time to put some syllables together!

BLEVIN: Whatever. Righto, chaps. Give me something metal, Marlowe.

MARLOWE: My command.

BLEVIN: Yo Yo Hey
They call me Razor cause I'll cut you
Red and white heaven rise above you

> Look at me dirty and I'll scrub you
> Didn't sign up for this so fuck you
> Fuck you and Fuck you, too
> Mic drop, I'm done, Fuck you

That's my verse, scrots. Half as long because I'm worth twice as much.

BRODY: Blevin is brief. A first.

BAGO: OK, OK. You almost got skills, Razor! Lookin better! [*beat*] I wouldn't cut, though. Nah.

[BAGO *and* BRODY *give each other pounds, laughing*]

BRODY: Not in a million, "Razor"!

BLEVIN: Excuse me?! Ugh. Here we go again. Marlowe, haven't we killed enough time? Where's this second car you promised?

BRODY: He told us—

MARLOWE: Why don't you choose a word game, Blevin? And we'll follow your lead.

BLEVIN: Ugh…

MARLOWE: Want to go for a walk? Change of venue?

BLEVIN: It's pitch black out there!

BAGO: Let's do Cypher round 2! Bagorocks is Iayze cool, like: "I like green tip 5-5-6 my A-R-Ps! I like pouring tris, fucking hoes—"

BLEVIN: No! No! No! No more rap crap. That ghetto shit is tiresome. I have a better idea. Two Truths and a Lie! ALL of us play, 5 questions; this time you too, Marlowe.

MARLOWE: OK. Challenge accepted.

BLEVIN: You sure? You haven't heard the conditions.

MARLOWE: They are?

BLEVIN: We get personal. Divulge some hidden shame. And Marlowe, since you're not a person—

BRODY: A cat is a person.

BLEVIN: Since you're not a human person, you proxy for The Foundation. Reveal something hidden from the public record. Unshroud the mystery of The Study's "landmark" research. Enlighten us as to the motives behind the modus operandi. We'll keep your confidence.

MARLOWE: I have no doubts.

BLEVIN: Oh! So you trust me?

MARLOWE: I didn't say that. [*beat*] Shall we begin?

BRODY: I am curious, Marlowe. Something seems to have shifted since our pick up.

MARLOWE: Perhaps.

BRODY: Are you keeping secrets?

MARLOWE: Are you?

BAGO: God, this is so boring! Let's play already!

BLEVIN: With shots. To loosen the tongues and lips. I know there's more tequila here somewhere.

BRODY: Porch.

BLEVIN: Do I have to move?

BRODY: Do your legs work?

BAGO: [*pulls a bottle of 1800 Tequila from between the sofa cushions*] Actually, there's…

BLEVIN: Thank you, JHC! Give me a little salt, lime, and some real music and we have a party.

BRODY: Oh…Miss Razor Trash wants to spice it up.

BLEVIN: I know how to party, Princess Bro.

BRODY: Obviously. Shows in the skin.

BAGO: Marlowe, how about pizza and beer? No, wait, let's smoke first.

MARLOWE: After we tell our tales, Bago.

BLEVIN: Yeah, Dino Bago, after the liquor and the lies.

BRODY: I'm more interested in the truths.

BLEVIN: I went for the alliteration.

BRODY: And the drama.

BLEVIN: Rich.

BRODY: Poor.

BAGO: If we don't do something, go somewhere, I'm gonna earl!

MARLOWE: Take the lead, Blevin.

BLEVIN: No. You lead, Marlowe. You brought us here.

BAGO: Jesus fucking Christ! Just fucking…Oh god…I need a blunt!

MARLOWE: Bago, sit.

BAGO: Sorry.

MARLOWE: Is anyone familiar with the parable of the wise assassin?

BLEVIN: Great. Numb nuts calls on Jesus and God so that's The Holy Cat's cue to wax sermonic.

MARLOWE: The Kingdom of the Father is like a certain man who wished to kill a tyrant. In his own house, the man drew his sword and thrust it into the wall to find out whether his hand could carry through. Then he slew the tyrant and washed both his hands in the blood.

The Property is like the Kingdom of the Father and they who sent me are like the Father.

BLEVIN: Riddles?

BRODY: Please speak plainly, Marlowe.

MARLOWE: The Foundation is the Father. The Study is the Sword. And I am the man.

BAGO: What the fuck?

MARLOWE: Four questions remain. Shall I continue?

BLEVIN: Spare us the riddles. Be candid.

MARLOWE: My words are unbiased and free from malice. There are no innocents here.

BRODY: Marlowe, what's happening?

MARLOWE: Your Majesty?

BRODY: Marlowe?

[*In fluid motion,* MARLOWE*'s neck elongates, their tail unfurls and their jaw relaxes.* MARLOWE*'s mouth falls open and* THE HIVE*'s voice emerges.*]

THE HIVE: Our fun.

[*The sound is a mushroom cloud flowering through the ceiling into the sky, a fluorescent sea of moss climbing down from the eaves to the walls of the house, a voracious colony of wasps migrating across the floor of the theater, a droning low tone. Fleeing the sting of vibration,* BAGO, BLEVIN, *and* BRODY *scramble to the isle of the sofa, pull their feet up, and tuck their legs beneath them.*]

BLEVIN: This isn't fun. And this isn't funny.

[MARLOWE *shudders, stretches and cracks their neck, resuming function as their body.* BAGO, BLEVIN, *and* BRODY *watch, listen, and feel the dull throb of* THE HIVE *in their muscles and bones. They want to move but find their bodies stiffening. Their mouths, nostrils, and ears fill as if under water.* THE HIVE, *the voice and personage of* THE FOUNDATION, *is fully present alongside and beneath them.*]

THE HIVE: It's our fun, not yours. We're just playing your game. [*beat*] Where were we? Oh. Candid. The Foundation is a hive mind and Marlowe is our voice and instrument—

MARLOWE: Though I would much prefer to be a cat.

THE HIVE: —our agent sent to acclimate you to the state of The Property, your new habitation.

MARLOWE: Mostly to loaf in the grass and watch the butterflies in the exquisite silence of my solitary thoughts.

THE HIVE: Your bodies are suspended in midair, joined by a shaft of light.

MARLOWE: [*sighs*] It's more like a spit through the spinal columns. From the crown of your head to the coccyx at the base of your spine.

THE HIVE: So you can make a contribution. This is the only way you will generate light, troubled as you are. Tortured.

MARLOWE: They have you threaded like a shish kebab. Tailbone to skull.

THE HIVE: There was no first car. No snow storm. No break down.

MARLOWE: Unfortunately—

THE HIVE: There's no tow. No second car. You have arrived.

MARLOWE: You'll last like this as long as the tubing does. Plastic so it won't biodegrade—

THE HIVE: The human mind is a many-splendored thing. Miraculous really.

MARLOWE: —but at some point it'll get brittle.

THE HIVE: It amuses itself.

MARLOWE: But it won't break unless you move which is highly unlikely—

THE HIVE: Needs only a little stimulus and a few suggestions.

MARLOWE: —something like point zero zero zero zero zero zero add more zeros zero zero percent chance.

THE HIVE: Had enough candid?

[*Together* BAGO, BLEVIN, *and* BRODY *jerk forward suddenly as if pulled or thrown. In unison they ease back into the sofa. Their eyes scan space. Their torsos shift in place. The air pulses.*]

THE HIVE: Nothing? Well, there was one of you who departed the scene. She was a liability.

MARLOWE: A light.

THE HIVE: A liability. A light. You insist on splitting hairs. Call it dawdle or tarry: No one who is anyone cares. Nothing ventured, nothing gained. Nothing risked, nothing learned. The deviation proves the rule. The Pith: She did not belong at The Property but her data out-values the expense.

BLEVIN: [*finds her tongue*] There was someone…else? With us?

THE HIVE: Strike that. Autocorrect! [*laughter*] [*beat*] Episodic memory has yet to be proven advantageous at The Property. We continue: There was no pickup. You've not left our company since your intake interview. Once you signed, you began being mined. The. End. Game.

BLEVIN: What the, what the actual fuck?! Scrots?!

[BAGO, BLEVIN, *and* BRODY *look at each other, whispering, and stealthily move their limbs to awaken them*]

MARLOWE: You really should read a legal document before you sign it. Attorneys for The Foundation are very thorough. Always.

BAGO: But that was like 500 pages. Of words.

BLEVIN: This fool.

THE HIVE: Words, diagrams, graphs, photos, and drawings.

BAGO: Huh?

BLEVIN: Brody? Please, if you will.

[*Beat*]

BRODY: Words and pictures, bro.

BAGO: Awwww…Fuck me, man.

THE HIVE: Marlowe?

MARLOWE: And multiple locations requiring your signature and/or initials. You were invited to take all the time you needed to review The Binder.

BLEVIN: It was, literally, 500 pages.

MARLOWE: Four hundred forty pages. And The Foundation recommended you bring counsel—

BLEVIN: Who the F had money for a lawyer?

MARLOWE: —Or consult The Attorneys during The Review.

BAGO: You said there was nothing to worry about.

MARLOWE: I wasn't there. The Attorneys—

BAGO: Somebody said it.

MARLOWE: —Were made available at no cost for the entirety of The Review Period.

BAGO: Said if we just signed, we could be outta there in 15 minutes.

MARLOWE: The Review Period is an indeterminate length. Participants are invited to peruse The Binder at their leisure.

BLEVIN: Oh Fuck ALL.

[*As if escaping a fire,* BAGO *dives from the sofa, rolls, and springs to his feet.* BLEVIN *and* BRODY *follow his lead. They all stand flailing a bit, disoriented.* BAGO *turns to run to the porch. It isn't there.*

Instead there is a an increasingly audible hum and a sweet chemical smell. All semblance of door, window, corridor, and exit is enveloped in a hard gauze, the room is a black box, a matte black cast.

BAGO *and* BLEVIN *look for the tequila. They find nothing.* BAGO *bites his nails, pacing.* BLEVIN *begins searching for her sketchbook and pencils.* BRODY *just leans on the sofa arm and shakes his head.*]

BRODY: Good lord. What have we done? Marlowe?

THE HIVE: You signed…

BRODY: Not you! Marlowe! A Cat!

[MARLOWE *lowers their head*]

THE HIVE: You may proceed.

MARLOWE: Yes, Your Majesty?

BRODY: Is this it?

BLEVIN: Why are you consulting their agent? This "cat" and that "foundation" are one corporate entity.

MARLOWE: I have my own desires, Blevin, and my own judgments.

BLEVIN: And your own motives. Your own deceit.

MARLOWE: No. [*to* BRODY] Your Majesty, while there's time. [*lifts their head, cocks it to the side*] I would offer, if I may, a reprieve.

THE HIVE: Another delay? [*beat*] Is your jury still out? We are unanimous. Speak now, we are also impatient. Relieve us of these 3 and their figurative squirming, refresh the game! Or shall we retreat?

MARLOWE: I assure you, some amusement yet remains. Look alive, my players! We'll have another round on the house!

BLEVIN: Round of what?! We're swimming in antifreeze and bleach. With a side of petrol.

BAGO: And hella gasoline.

THE HIVE: Oh, look alive while you're yet alive to look! Or don't.

[*Beat*]

Ah. They are subdued.

Marlowe, speak!! We tire quickly.

MARLOWE: I say we finish Blevin's game—give them their chance: 2 truths and a lie—and then decide.

THE HIVE: You have abandoned your post and are far afield. But what is this new sensation? It feels [*beat*] light. You, Marlowe, intrigue. This is data.

MARLOWE: [*with their eyes locked with* BRODY'*s*] And the game? They were duped.

THE HIVE: And? Their suffering is a temporary amusement that can be aroused in an instant. Everything they experience we allow. The House wins.

MARLOWE: Raised stakes. One player. One truth.

THE HIVE: Hmph.

MARLOWE: Conditions of the game. Their memories will be wiped.

THE HIVE: Hmph.

MARLOWE: My memory will be wiped.

THE HIVE: Absurd and wasteful.

MARLOWE: I will only observe, will not participate in the construct.

THE HIVE: Concern with conditions of the game is imbecilic. What are the stakes?

MARLOWE: If they lose, you mine this new sensation—my…light.

THE HIVE: Marlowe! This is a fool's errand. We will mine your light regardless.

MARLOWE: Liberty or death.

BAGO: Man, fuck all that.

BRODY: Bago! Quiet!

THE HIVE: Liberty or death. And we lose our investment and the return? Bah humbug. [*laughter*]

MARLOWE: If they lose, you accompany me within them and I step aside for you to observe the interiors without mediation.

THE HIVE: Again, you offer us a prize that is already ours. [*laughter*] You are becoming human. Desperation does not suit you. Ahhhh.

[*Beat*]

Enough bartering, Benefactor! These are the terms: One question. One player. One truth. If they succeed: A chance to earn embodied liberty and a natural death. Or, should failure be their constant companion: exhaustive mining in perpetuity or until we run out of plastic—whichever comes first.

BLEVIN: I'm going to be sick.

MARLOWE: OK.

THE HIVE: Until they are fully restored and attend an exit interview at a location later specified, all data and energy mining will continue as per the original agreement henceforth, from this day forward, etcetera, etcetera.

MARLOWE: Agreed. The question?

THE HIVE: We will observe from the velarium. And elsewhere. Enjoy the breeze.

[*The low tone and sweet smell fade sharply as* THE FOUNDATION *retreats.* BRODY *and* BAGO *shudder.* BLEVIN *retches and dry heaves.* MARLOWE, A CAT *stretches to their full length, appearing now even larger, with darker fur, and a heavier brow. They speak slowly, almost as if to whisper.*]

MARLOWE: Post-haste. Raised stakes. That went well.

BAGO: Oh yeah. This is bad.

BRODY: Yep.

BLEVIN: Holy Effin Eff.

MARLOWE: One question. One Player. One truth. Who will play?

BLEVIN: My guts might have been churning in my ears but, um, what is the question?

BAGO: It could be anything. Like, how long have we been here? What time is it really? Who is the President of the United States of America?

BRODY: Or that could be the question: What's the question?

BAGO: Oh…yeahhhhhh. Dude. Bro. We need weed.

BLEVIN: Single malt whiskey.

BRODY: Prayer.

MARLOWE: The question is not the issue. Who will answer?

BLEVIN: Dear emotional-support-muck-a-muck: Which of us should answer, depends on the question. We need to strategize.

BRODY: I agree with Blevin.

BAGO: Yeah. We gotta be on some three musketeers shit now, cat.

MARLOWE: It doesn't work like that. I cannot reveal the question until the group chooses the player. And it must be a consensus choice: unanimous. One cohort, one player, one voice.

BLEVIN: One truth.

BAGO: Mane. This shit is crazy. I got no weed, no drink, no pills, no music: I'm sober as fuck and I don't know what's true. These alien vampire mugs got us like skewered meat, dog. I have no plan for this shit here. I got nothing. I mean. Fuck. Maybe we just go back to waiting on the tow.

BRODY: That shit is not coming, man! It's all ruined. We got played like…I don't have words.

BLEVIN: Me either.

BAGO: Word.

[*Beat*]

[*They all laugh. Deep belly, rolling on the floor laughter. And tears.*]

BLEVIN: So, Marlowe, I want to say…

MARLOWE: It's OK, Blevin. You don't have to apologize.

BLEVIN: I wasn't going to.

MARLOWE: I know. I still have access to your profiles. And your thoughts.

BAGO: So…hold up, G. If you know what we're thinking, why do you talk to us out loud?

MARLOWE: You don't know what I'm thinking, Bago.

BAGO: Right, that's why I'm asking you why.

BLEVIN: [*shakes her head and rolls her eyes in palpable disbelief*] OK, Queen B, it's you or me.

[*Beat*]

BAGO: What? That's a pretty serious question I'm asking and I think it deserves an answer!

BRODY: Just keep thinking at it, Bago. It will give you something new to do. Unless there's a hole card we don't know abouwt, we all have to find ourselves a hobby for the next…Umph…My mind is racing. How is this place suddenly dry as the desert?

The devil comes through and lays these heavy truths on us like hellfire rugs and don't even leave us salve for the wounds. That's the truth I got to share! Doomed, bitches, we are doomed if I have to step up to the mic. So.

Ms. Blevin Trash Razor, girl. No tea, no shade, it's all Box Wine. You're
Shakespeare's sister: you're the one with the 100,000 dollar words! I'm
just a small town queen sipping on lean. For true. It's on you, baby!

BLEVIN: Seems like it's on you, Queen. You're the one with story every-
one loves, Brody. Especially, Marlowe. I can't remember a rat's ass or a
chicken's shit about that story but Marlowe is the closest thing we have
to The Foundation genie, so I'd bet real money on that tale. Not that
I have any.

BRODY: Not that you need any. Look at us! But, heck, Minnie Pearl that
story is not going to save us.

MARLOWE: I beg to differ. Admittedly, nothing is going to save you out-
right. I did my best to nudge you toward the light, but your inclinations—

BRODY: —Are toward the shade. Touché, pussycat.

BLEVIN: So we just endure until our bodies fall apart?

MARLOWE: No. I think the snow story is the key. Or one of them. There
are a series of doors. However it is, we need to act soon before The Hive
changes its mind.

BRODY: I don't see how my kiddy dream, about an angel with my sister's
face saving me from freezing to death in the woods, is the key to jack.

MARLOWE: I can't say anything more. I may have said too much already.
Just… Come to an agreement. One voice, one player, one truth. Your
cohort trusts you. Right Blevin? Right Bago?

BAGO: I know I don't know shit and flip a coin tween y'all two but if Cat
says you the man, Broho, my bands are on you.

BLEVIN: Right, like that.

BRODY: The Queen B is in deep with no tea and no D. [*beat*] Fuck.

MARLOWE: Nothing to lose. Everything to gain.

[BRODY *closes his eyes and massages his temples with his fingertips. He breathes
deeply but makes no motion to speak.*]

BAGO: [*to no one in particular*] I can't feel my legs.

BLEVIN: [*ignores* BAGO] So what does he do? Just tell it again?

BAGO: My hands don't feel right.

MARLOWE: [*ignores* BAGO] Not exactly.

BLEVIN: Then what's the trick?

BAGO: Like I got spiders crawling in my shit.

MARLOWE: [*to* BRODY] Nothing. Here. Is as simple. As it seems.

BAGO: And ice icicles in my neck.

BLEVIN: Tell me something I don't know.

MARLOWE: That's up to Brody. Your Majesty?

BAGO: Something don't smell right.

BRODY: [*to* MARLOWE] What part do I tell?

BAGO: Maybe I'm not real!

MARLOWE: Tell it all. The whole menagerie. Each nuance and shade.

BAGO: Heyyy! Heyyyyy! Fuckkkk!

[*Beat*]

MARLOWE: It starts innocently enough.

BAGO: Heyyyyyyy, can you see me? Am I—

[MARLOWE *steps in front of* BAGO, *places their front paws upon* BAGO*'s chest.* BAGO*'s body goes limp. He smiles faintly. He is fast asleep.*]

MARLOWE: [*positions* BAGO *gently on the sofa*] Beauty sleep and bliss. For the quick and the dead. You are of one accord. Unfold your truth. No further interruptions. No discussion or dissent can fortune bear or bury.

[BLACK OUT]

CONTRIBUTORS

SEBASTIÁN CALDERÓN BENTIN is a theater artist and Associate Professor in the Department of Drama at the Tisch School of the Arts, New York University. He has performed Jay Wright's work in collaboration with Chicago-based theater company Every House Has a Door, including *The Three Matadors* (2017), based on a micro-play embedded in Wright's book-length poem *The Presentable Art of Reading Absence* (Dalkey Archive Press, 2008), and more recently, a staged reading of the first ten pages of the play *Passage* (2022), included in the anthology *Selected Plays of Jay Wright Volume I: The Dramatic Radiance of Number* (Kenning Editions, 2022).

MICHAEL BERLIN is a writer and educator living in Charlottesville, VA. His writing has appeared or is forthcoming in *Cultural Critique*, *The Georgia Review*, *Jewish Currents*, and *Early Modern Cultural Studies*.

WILL DADDARIO is a scholar, teacher, grief worker, and mental health counselor. He is the author of the following books: with Matthew Goulish, *Pitch and Revelation: reconfigurations of reading, poetry, and philosophy through the work of Jay Wright* (Punctum); *Baroque, Venice, Theatre, Philosophy* (Springer 2017). He has also edited: with Harry Wilson, *Rethinking Roland Barthes through Performance: A Desire for Neutral Dramaturgy* (Bloomsbury/Methuen, 2023); with Karoline Gritzner, *Adorno and Performance* (Palgrave, 2014); with Laura Cull Ó Maoilearca, *Manifesto Now! Instructions for Performance, Philosophy, Politics* (Intellect, 2013). He is a founding member of Performance Philosophy and co-editor of that group's book series (with Rowman and Littlefield) and peer-reviewed online journal (performancephilosophy.org/journal). With his wife, Joanne Zerdy, he provides workshops and online classes through Inviting Abundance in Asheville, NC.

DAVID GRUBBS is Professor of Music at Brooklyn College and The Graduate Center, CUNY. He is the author of *Good night the pleasure was ours, The Voice in the Headphones, Now that the audience is assembled,* and *Records Ruin the Landscape: John Cage, the Sixties, and Sound Recording* (all published by Duke University Press) as well as the collaborative artists' books *Simultaneous Soloists* (with Anthony McCall, Pioneer Works Press) and *Projectile* (with Reto Geiser and John Sparagana, Drag City). As a musician, Grubbs has released fourteen solo albums and appeared on more than 200 releases.

Performance artist and scholar DURIEL E. HARRIS is the author of three critically acclaimed volumes of poetry: *Drag* (2003); *Amnesiac: Poems* (2010); and *No Dictionary of a Living Tongue* (Nightboat, 2017), finalist for the Audre Lorde Award. Multi-genre works include the one-woman theatrical performance *Thingification*, the videopoem collaboration *Speleology*, and the conceptual sound-image project *Blood Labyrinth*. Appearances include performances at the Greenhouse Theater, the Chicago Jazz Festival, Naropa, Babylon Cinema (Berlin), Votive (Auckland), Babel Theatre (Beirut), the Art Institute of Chicago, and the Festival Internacional de Poesía de La Habana. Her work has been featured in the *New York Times*, BAX, *Letters to the Future, Of Poetry and Protest*, the *&Now Awards, Imagined Theatres*, PEN America, and Poets.org, among others. Harris is Professor of English at Illinois State University and Editor of the award-winning publishing platform Obsidian: Literature & Arts in the African Diaspora.

DEVIN KING is writing a biography of Ronald Johnson. He is the author most recently of *Gathering* (Kenning Editions, 2023). He lives in Oxford, England.

MATTHEW GOULISH co-founded *Every house has a door* in 2008 with director Lin Hixson. He is a dramaturge and performer for the company. His books include *39 microlectures: in proximity of performance* (Routledge, 2001), *The Brightest Thing in the World: 3 Lectures from the Institute of Failure* (Green Lantern Press, 2012), *Work from Memory: In Response to In Search of Lost Time by Marcel Proust*, co-authored with Dan Beachy-Quick (Ahsahta Press, 2012) and *Pitch and Revelation: Reconfigurations of Reading, Poetry, and Philosophy through the Work of Jay Wright*, co-authored with Will Daddario (Punctum Books, 2022). He teaches in the Writing Program of The School of the Art Institute of Chicago.

ESTEBAN RODRÍGUEZ is the author of eight poetry collections, most recently *Lotería* (Texas Review Press, 2023), and the essay collection *Before the Earth Devours Us* (Split/Lip Press, 2021). He is the Interviews Editor for the *EcoTheo Review*, Senior Book Reviews Editor for *Tupelo Quarterly*, and Associate Poetry Editor for *AGN*. He lives with his family in south Texas.

DANIEL WOODY earned his Master of Fine Arts in Writing from the School of the Art Institute of Chicago. He currently works as Clinical Assistant Professor at New York University's portal campus in Shanghai, China, where he teaches courses in poetry and academic writing. His own poetry can be found in *Chicago Review*, *The Journal Petra*, *Volta*, and elsewhere. He is currently at work on a hybrid genre manuscript about Chinese tea and poetry.

SELECTED BACKLIST

Hieroglyphs of the Inverted World, by Rob Halpern

The Science of Departures, by Adalber Salas Hernández,
translated by Robin Myers

título / title, by Legna Rodríguez Iglesias,
translated by Katherine M. Hedeen

The Kenning Anthology of Poets Theater: 1945–1985,
edited by David Brazil and Kevin Killian

Stage Fright: Plays from San Francisco Poets Theater, by Kevin Killian

Gathering, by Devin King

Zeroes Were Hollow, by David Larsen

Tomatoes, by Nathalie Quintane,
translated by Marty Hiatt, foreword by Juliana Spahr

Festivals of Patience: The Verse Poems of Arthur Rimbaud,
translated by Brian Kim Stefans, foreword by Jennifer Moxley

The Dirty Text, by Soleida Ríos,
translated by Barbara Jamison and Olivia Lott

Grenade in Mouth: Some Poems of Miyó Vestrini, edited by Faride Mereb,
translated by Anne Boyer and Cassandra Gillig

Hannah Weiner's Open House, by Hannah Weiner,
edited with a foreword by Patrick Durgin

Coronavirus Haiku, by Worker Writers School,
edited and foreword by Mark Nowak

The Dramatic Radiance of Number: Selected Plays of Jay Wright, Volume 1

Figurations and Dedications: Selected Plays of Jay Wright, Volume 2

kenningeditions.com